Sourdough Breads and Coffee Cakes

104 Recipes Using Homemade Starters

by Ada Lou Roberts

Drawings by Francoise Webb

Dover Publications, Inc.
New York

Published in Canada by General Publishing Company, Ltd., 30 Lesmill Road, Don Mills, Toronto, Ontario.
Published in the United Kingdom by Constable and Company, Ltd., 10 Orange Street, London WC2H 7EG.

This Dover edition, first published in 1983, is an unabridged republication of *Breads and Coffee Cakes with Homemade Starters from Rose Lane Farm*, originally published by Hearthside Press, Inc., in 1967. The Sources of Supply section has been updated.

Manufactured in the United States of America
Dover Publications, Inc., 31 East 2nd Street, Mineola, N.Y. 11501

Library of Congress Cataloging in Publication Data

Roberts, Ada Lou.
  Sourdough Breads and Coffee Cakes.

  Reprint. Originally published: Breads and coffee cakes with homemade starters from Rose Lane Farm. New York : Hearthside Press, 1967. With minor updated corrections.
  Bibliography: p.
  Includes index.
  1. Bread.   I. Title.
TX769.R63   1983   641.8′15   83-5260
ISBN 0-486-24529-2

*This book is dedicated to the memory of my mother,
Sarah Emma Hastings Stillinger, who, during her
lifetime, baked mountains of bread for a large
family, and many hired men and numerous relatives
who lived in our home from time to time.*

Acknowledgement

Portions of the material in the first six chapters and my recipes for Potato Bread Starter, Saint Nicholas Bread, Snap, Crackle, Pop Bread, Soy and Sorghum Bread, Gossip Tea Bread, Scotch Oatmeal Bread, Parsnip Bread, Spiced Rye Bread and Chestnut Bread are reprinted by courtesy of *Gourmet Magazine*.

Contents

Heritage in Spice

Some things the years do not erase:
The Evening Star above
Comes back steadily at dusk
To remind me of
The quiet way she let us know
The largess of her love.

The wooden spoon and mixing bowl
Were all that had to show,
We knew her hands would soon be
            kneading
Balls of velvet dough,
How eagerly we waited for
The yeast to make it grow.

Strange that I remember most,
Though memories come in droves,
Her hovering hands like benisons
Above the honeyed loaves,
Dusting a scented heritage
Of cinnamon and cloves.

JESSIE FARNHAM
(Reproduced courtesy of MRS. CHARLES FARNHAM
and CURTIS PUBLISHING COMPANY.)

Here Is a Miracle

Making bread is such a pleasant task
When the children come to ask,
"Mother, where's a roll, where's a bun?'"
Then it is always so much fun
To set out bowl, sifter, yeast and flour.
It gives one such a feeling of power
To take these simple things
And create this miracle called bread.

I think of the time when there was no bread.
What did the woman do when the children said,
"Mother, we are hungry," and they cried?
Then such a woman for the first time tried
And, searching the hills and the valleys, found
The seeds; then learning they could be ground,
She baked flat cakes of water and meal
In the ashes to still the children's cries.

I think of my mother with a family to feed.
She no longer needed to grind the seed,
Still breadmaking took a heavy toll of time.
How many loaves she produced! Such a line
Of white and brown and rye for many
People sat at our table in those days,
Passing the bread, eating their fill
With never the thought—Here is a miracle.

I think of the children today with thin arms
Outstretched, crying for grain from our farms.
I wish there was bread to bake for them all,
That they, too, could grow fine and firm and tall.
What a common, common thing for us,
What a miracle to those who have it not.
If I could make a wish for all the world—
Give them bread. Let the basket never be empty.

ADA LOU ROBERTS

1
Breads Then and Now

Now that sourdough breads have become luxury items, traveling by air to arrive fresh for sale in gourmet shops across the country, or by mail to individual customers who are charged five dollars for two loaves, I would like to share my collection of recipes for breads made from "barm," "ferment" or "starter," whichever term you prefer. I like "starter" best.

Early bakers had a picturesque trade language, as well as many peculiar beliefs concerning methods of carrying on their work. Had one happened to hear a group of them discussing their problems it might have been suspected that they were talking about some capricious woman. They used such words as "quick," "flighty," "flying," "blooming," "anemic," "claggy," "foxy," "overwrought" and "virgin," to name just a few. These words show us that breadmaking then was far from the uniform, controlled process that it is today—and that is what makes the history of baking such a fascinating subject.

There is no doubt that bread was truly the staff of life for many centuries after it was discovered. One leading baker even set forth in his writing that the personality of the people of a certain section or even a whole country was affected by the quality of the bread which they ate. He used Scotland as an example, saying that when people were fed on bread of a heavy, sour, sodden nature they were bound to be dour, plodding and frugal, implying heavily that the people of England with their light, fine, white bread were more cheerful, brisk and generous.

One book on breadmaking defines bread simply as "dough made from flour and water and usually made to ferment by the addition of yeast." But a crumbling old baker's guide informs us that "the object of baking is to combine the gluten and the starch of the flour into a homogeneous substance and to excite such vimous fermentative action by means of its saccharine matter as shall disengage an abundance of carbon acid gas in it for making an agreeable, soft, succulent sponge and easily digestible loaf." (Succulent seems to me a very odd adjective to apply here.) In spite of the difference in language between the centuries, the principals of breadmaking have remained essentially the same but the preferences of the peoples of the world have caused frequent changes in the kinds of flour used.

Researchers have been able to piece together a more complete history of bread than of any other food now known to man. Many interesting books to be found in public libraries and private collections give details of the progress of the baking industry through the ages. Later in this book I give a list of those on my own shelves which I have found particularly interesting and from which I have gained many ideas for my work.

From the time of the supposedly accidental discovery of the fermentation process in Egypt, it seems that every product of garden and field with a little starch and/or fiber to help hold a loaf together has been used in bread at one time or another. Some were used to make the bread better but many, such as straw, were used merely as a filler, to increase the volume, by poor bakers who found it hard to make a profit on their products even though for many years the governments of some countries forbade the practice of baking at home. At one time, lower-class people in Britain were not allowed to have ovens in their houses and so were forced to take even their meats to the public bakeries for roasting. Later the housewife was allowed to go or send to the bakery for a measure of yeast, make up the bread herself at home, and when it was "proved" carry it back to the shop to be baked. When the finished loaves were picked up the owner could not always be sure that she was getting back her own loaves and, since the reason for mixing it at home was to make sure that the dough was not adulterated, many ingenious ways of marking loaves were devised by the thrifty cottager.

A fascinating little book, *Cottage Economy* by William Cobbett of England, evidently quite popular because it was first published in 1821 and was still being reprinted in a 17th edition in 1850, contains a vigorous sermon urging laboring-class people to take care of their baking at home for reasons of both economy and health. He states flatly that, "Every woman, high or low, ought to know how to make bread. If she do not, she is unworthy of trust and confidence, and, indeed, a mere burden upon the community! Yet, it is a sad thing that many women seem to know nothing about bread other than the part which belongs to its consumption." Mr. Cobbett was a large land-owner and, to put his beliefs into action, he always asked a prospective tenant if his wife could bake. If she could not, there was no chance of her husband being hired. Mr. Cobbett figured that not only would a baking wife be worth a pound or two more to the family in savings, but that the husband would be worth more to him for, being better nourished, he would be able to do more and better work. He was dead set against the substitution of "Ireland's lazy root" (potatoes) for bread in the laborer's diet and prayed for the day when "we shall once more see the knife in the labourer's hand and the loaf upon the board." He also was vigorous in his campaign against the government tax on malt and full of suggestions for the people to raise their own grain, at least enough to make their own malt, on their small plots of land.

Strange ideas were held about some of the combinations of grains used. For instance, it was thought that "maslin" bread, made from a mixture of rye and wheat raised together on the same soil, then harvested, ground and sifted together, was much better than that made from equal quantities of pure rye and wheat from separate fields, and people were willing to pay a premium for it.

History is said to repeat itself but, in the case of the greatly renewed interest in bread, the repeat is in a somewhat reversed order. Today those who can afford the best are looking for the old, home-style breads containing wholesome grain flours and meals. In early days fine white bread was a status symbol, so much so that as the upper-class people demanded whiter and whiter loaves with finer and still finer texture, the bakers used a number of harmful additives to secure these results until in the middle of the eighteenth century, a campaign was begun to abolish the use of alum, marble dust, carbonate of lead, blue vitriol and other chemicals which doctors claimed were ruining the health of the entire population of London as well as affecting all the country.

About this time a wheat shortage caused the government to authorize production of a standard loaf containing a higher proportion of bran. The liquid obtained from soaking bran in warm water was believed to increase the yield from each batch of bread mixed. Doctors began to endorse the use of other grains such as millet, barley and oats but, for the most part, the people were not impressed. There continued to be "white" bakers and "brown" bakers, with legal controls as to the grades of bread which they could produce. There was much rivalry between the baking guilds, with shows to exhibit their whitest, finest-textured loaves. One winner was reported to have run a batch of dough through the rollers thirty-six times to produce the first prize loaf, but the taster sadly declared that all the flavor had been lost in the process.

In Scotland the finest white bread, known as "manchet," was reserved for royalty and the great landlords. "Cheat," the second finest grade, was found in the homes of the upper-class trades-men. "Raveled" bread was made from the whole grain flour just as it came from the mill to be consumed by the country folk and villagers just above the servant class. "Mashloch" was baked for the very poor and the servants. It contained only coarse bran mixed with rye. In the great houses the mistress or housekeeper carried the keys to the food safes where the fine bread and best grades of other food were kept to avoid tempting the servants to acquire a taste for the higher priced products. Later, the govern-ment passed a law requiring the brown bakers to add a certain percent of wheat germ to the mashloch to improve the health of the working class.

Bakers for the aristocracy looked down on the brown bakers with sneering contempt. One member of a London Upper Guild was quoted as saying that he supposed a sort of bread could be made from the coarse stuff (which brown bakers used), in-timating that it really should not be dignified with the name of bread. He added that he had heard of a bread-corn being fre-quently employed in America but surely it could never make a good loaf bread. Oh, how wrong he was! There is no more at-tractive and satisfying bread made than a golden-crusted loaf containing the proper proportions of corn meal and wheat flour.

Perhaps it was this same skeptic who reported hearing rumors of a mechanical bread mixer being used in this country. He predicted positively that such contraptions would never come into general use in good trade, for fine bread must always be made by hand. Well, they certainly did come into general use but I agree with him that the best bread must still be made by hand. Furthermore, there is a great sense of satisfaction when one learns to recognize the signs that the dough has reached the proper stage for working to obtain the best results.

Finally, I want to give you a sample of some of the recipes from my precious old books in the hopes that it will inspire you to search out and read every old cookbook you can find. It will add greatly to your enjoyment of baking for your family.

Some Interesting Old Recipes

This recipe for making yeast with hops is taken from *Enquire Within upon Everything*, an old English book which came to me by way of Australia, but it compares almost word for word with one purported to have been written in an album by Calamity Jane to let her daughter know that she had also been a good cook in her days in the wild West.

"Boil, say on Monday morning, 2 ozs. of the best hops in 4 quarts of water for half an hour; strain it and let the liquor cool to new-milk warmth, then put in a small handful of salt, and half a pound of sugar. Beat up one pound of the best flour with some of the liquor and then mix all well together. On Wednesday add three pounds of potatoes boiled and then mashed, to stand until Thursday. Then strain it, put into bottles and it is ready to use. It must be stirred frequently while in the making and kept near the fire. Before using shake the bottle well. It will keep in a cool place for two months and is best the later part of the period. This yeast ferments spontaneously, not requiring the aid of other yeast and, if care is taken that it ferment well in the earthen bowl in which it was made, you may cork it up tight when bottled. The quantity above will give four seltzer bottles full."

The following recipe for making bread comes from *Domestic Cookery*, also English. The copy which I have was given to a Canadian woman as a wedding gift in 1864.

"To make bread let flour be kept four to five weeks before it is begun to be used to bake with. Put half a bushel of good flour into a trough or kneading tub; mix with it between four and five quarts of warm water and a pint and a half of good hop yeast. Stir well with your hands until it becomes tough. Let it rise about an hour and a half or less if it rises fast; then, before it falls, add four more quarts of warm water and a half pound of salt. Work it well and cover with a cloth. Put the fire then into the oven and by the time it is warm enough the dough will be ready. Make the loaves about five pounds each; sweep out the oven very clean and quick, and put in the bread; shut it up close and two and one half hours will bake it. In summer the water should be milk warm, in winter a little more and in frosty weather as hot as you can well bear your hands in but not scalding else the whole will be ruined. If baked in tins the crust will be very nice.

"The oven should be round, not long; the roof twenty to twenty-four inches high, the mouth small and the door of iron to shut close. This construction will save firing and time and bake better than long and high-roofed ovens."

The same book tells how to preserve yeast.

"When you have plenty of yeast begin to save it in the following manner; whisk it until it becomes thin, then take a new, large wooden dish, wash it very nicely and when quite dry, lay a layer of yeast over the inside with a soft brush. Let it dry, then put another layer in the same manner and do so until you have sufficient quantity, observing that each coat dry thoroughly before another be added. It may be put on two to three inches thick and will keep for several months. When it is to be used, cut a piece out; stir it into warm water.

"If it is to be used for brewing, keep it by dipping large handfuls of birch twigs tied together and when dry repeat the dipping once. Take care that no dust come to them. When a wort is set to work, throw into it one of these bunches and it will do as well as with fresh yeast."

2

The Craft of Bread Baking

About the Starters

My first book, *Favorite Breads from Rose Lane Farm,* contained only one recipe for homemade starter and for making plain white bread with it. Soon after it came out I began to wonder, because of the deluge of mail, if I had not made a mistake in not devoting the whole book to breads made with starters. I appreciated so much the many ideas I got from the letters and from the people who came to call, hoping to beg, borrow or buy a cup of starter like Mother or Grandmother used to make—which they were too timid to initiate themselves—that I started to work on this collection of recipes. I sometimes had three jars of starter in the refrigerator at one time so that I could compare the results of one with the other in baking the same kinds of bread. I cannot say that I have a favorite. I like them all for one reason or another.

In planning the order in which to present the recipes it seemed best to place those for breads made with the Grated Raw Potato Starter first for two reasons. If you have never made starter breads these have built-in insurance in the form of the added package of dry yeast. This enables one to learn how starters work without nervousness about the process. Second, this starter is renewed each time a batch of bread is made, which may seem like a great convenience to the beginner. (Old-timers like myself, who have used starters for years, find it no trouble to renew any of them whenever necessary.)

Peach Leaf Dry Yeast Starter can be substituted for Grated Raw Potato Starter and renewed in the same way. The Peach Leaf Starter, Beer Starter, Ginger Beer Starter and Hop Starter can all be used interchangeably in the section of bread recipes following that for Hop Starter. The method of preparing the starter sponge in the evening may seem odd but this is the way I was told it was always done in a family which had kept the same starter going without a break for many years. I enjoyed doing it this way; the results were good, and so I did not experiment with any other method for this type of starter.

I am sure that each one who learns to use and enjoy starters will soon be doing his or her own experimenting with methods and combinations of ingredients.

Temperature

In working with starter breads remember to keep the temperature as uniform as possible (80 to 85 degrees) during both the fermentation of the starter and the rising of the dough. If, for any reason beyond your control, such as a pilot light going out or someone leaving a door open during the night (this has happened with me), the starter is not as active as it should be when you are ready to mix the dough, simply dissolve 1 package of dry yeast in ¼ cup warm water and add to the starter if you are making up one of the recipes which do not call for the yeast anyway. You will need to work in a little more flour as you knead it. If the recipe already uses yeast, additional yeast will not be needed. (All of the dried commercial starters I have tried call for the addition of dry yeast in their recipes, but this is not necessary with homemade starters, except to boost the action when something has slowed it down.)

Storing the Starter

Keep the stored starter at an even temperature (about 38 degrees F.) and it will keep for an indefinite period. I have found no deterioration even when I was unable to use any for three weeks, but if your starter should have a sharper aroma than you care for, after it has been stored for longer than usual, the remedy is simple: just sift ½ teaspoon soda and ½ teaspoon cream of tartar with 1 cup of the flour, add to the dough and proceed as usual.

Keep the storage jar for the starter very clean by scalding and airing well each time it is emptied and do use a large enough jar to allow for some expansion, just in case the refrigerator should cease to function for a long enough period so that the starter foams.

Overnight or Daytime Baking?

I have used the overnight method consistently in making these starter breads because I like to have my baking finished by noon. A woman whose working schedule is the exact opposite of mine, doing most of her cooking during the later part of the day, sets the sponge early in the morning and completes the baking in the evening. The results are just as good and could be even better if it is hard to maintain an even temperature during the night. The process can be shortened too by having everything just comfortably warm to the hand when mixing the sponge in the morning: mixing bowl, liquid, and flour. Do the same when mixing dough. Be sure that everything is warm—eggs, shortening, fruit, nuts or anything else which the recipe calls for. If you have an oven with pilot light, the pans, flour and other ingredients can be set in it while the sponge rises.

Flour

Wheat berries contain about 85 percent endosperm, 13 percent bran and 2 percent germ. After thousands of years of steady improvement in the milling processes, the millers of today with all their remarkable methods and machinery still are unable to extract the maximum amount of flour from these berries, and the search for more efficient methods continues. Even if it is not finished, the history of milling is a fascinating story, and well worth the effort to find books about the wonderful product which is so much a part of our daily life. Reading such a comprehensive volume as *Flour for Man's Bread*, with its striking illustrations, gives one a real appreciation for the contents of that sack on the cupboard shelf to which we hardly give a thought as we sift and stir and knead.

I am sure that cooks would enjoy their baking even more if they really understood the composition of flour, and how the elements work to provide us with the good results we hope for each time we mix a batch of bread. Also a knowledge of the differences between flours from various grains helps one to work out recipes tailored to individual preferences and thus affords even more pleasure from bread baking.

The baking quality of a flour depends mostly on the quantity and quality of the gluten content, or, more specifically, the two elements gliadin and glutenin. They combine in the breadmaking process to form gluten, which has the power to expand and hold the gases, thus controlling the lightness of the loaf. Some glutens have a much higher rate of expansion than others, so that the miller must make tests and blend different flours in order to effect the most efficient combination of elements.

Substituting Kinds of Flour

Wheat and rye are actually the only two grains containing enough expansion capability to permit making fine aerated bread. A general rule for using all other flours is to substitute them for about one-fourth the total amount of *wheat* flour called for in the recipe and, when using them, combine with only the best grade of wheat flour. Of course, if your preference is for a different texture than these proportions give, adjust the amounts to suit your own taste.

Whole-wheat, graham and cracked wheat (this should be covered with hot liquid and allowed to soak for a period of time before mixing) may be used interchangeably. Barley flour and rye may be substituted for each other when used with best quality white flour. Barley was prized for having extraordinary keeping qualities in early days. Scandinavians made a very thin bread (flatbrod) of barley and oats combined, which improved with age and was sometimes kept for thirty, forty or even more, years.

Toasting Flour

The English "baked" flour for making infants' first biscuits or cookies, and so when an unripe order of flour was received for regular use it was also given the oven treatment to improve its flavor. Do try it sometime. It does not take long and it does give the bread a rich, toasty flavor. Just take the amount of flour required, spread in shallow baking pan, place in 300°F. oven and watch carefully. Stir frequently and as soon as it begins to have a faint bisque tint remove from oven and cool before making into dough.

If Results Are Poor

In this day of controlled production one might think there would be no reason to give a thought to the quality of even the less expensive, regional brands of flour. This is not always true. Recently I saw the results of two bakings from the same sack of flour. The baker, who has been an excellent cook for many years, told me that the dough remained stringy and without proper body in spite of adding extra flour and longer kneading period. The dough was slow to rise and never did double in bulk. The baked rolls had poorly browned crust and pulled apart raggedly; the crumb had a dingy, yellowish tint. Weak gluten, insufficiently aged flour or that which has deteriorated in storage will give such results.

Storing Flour

Proper storage of the grain and the flour all along the way to your kitchen is important. After it reaches your kitchen it should not be set where it will become damp or absorb objectionable odors nor where it will be accessible to insects. I order a supply of varied flours and meals, which I cannot obtain locally, during the winter. I repack them in double plastic sacks and store in the freezer for use during the summer with never an ounce of loss.

Flour vs. Recipe

Experiment with the brand of flour which you use to find out whether it has the same powers of absorption as that used in the recipes in your cookbooks. When I suggest this to women who are having trouble with their baking, some tell me that they cannot afford to waste foodstuffs for their grocery bills are far too high as it is. There will be no waste if you experiment in the following manner: First, compare recipes from several sources for the same type of bread. When you have figured the average proportions of liquid to flour make up one of these recipes. If it calls for, say, 2 cups liquid to 5 cups flour, then take 1 cup of the liquid (use 2-cup measure) and add 1 cup of flour at a time making note of the increase in volume. Two nationally known brands of flour, between which I can find no difference, take 1 cup of flour to 1 cup of water to make 1½ cups dough, 2 cups flour to 1 cup water increases the volume to 2 cups. That is to say, the addition of each cup of flour to 1 cup of water increases the volume by ½ cup. Then 1 cup of water and 1 cup of flour make a pourable batter, 1 cup of water and 2 cups of flour make a soft spoonable dough and 1 cup of water and 2⅓ to 2½ cups of flour give a kneadable dough. 1 cup water to 3 cups flour makes a stiff dough which is apt to crack and be very dry when baked.

If your experiment gives the above results, then your flour may be used in the amounts given. If more or less is needed, adjust the amount of flour you need to give the right consistency, spoonful by spoonful, as you knead the dough (it is easy to add more flour but much harder to soften a too-stiff dough). The test dough you have now stirred up in your mixing bowl may be added to the rest of the ingredients in your mixing bowl and your baking completed. Not a spoonful of anything is wasted.

When you check a recipe, remember you must take into account all of the ingredients which contain some liquid in figuring the proportions, such as eggs, syrups, fruits, etc. This is one of the reasons why flour amounts must be approximate for most recipes, since the size of the eggs used, the type of syrup, and the amount of moisture retained by different types of potatoes and many other ingredients can make a difference of from a spoonful in a small recipe to perhaps a cupful in a large one.

This general knowledge of proportions will help you to detect mistakes more quickly when you look over a recipe. It seems that it is practically impossible to print a cookbook without a few mistakes. I can give you some examples I have come across recently in books just off the press. One calls for 4 cups flour in a small recipe for pancakes. Obviously not more than 2 cups of flour at the most could be used to make a pourable batter with the 1 cup of liquid and 1 egg called for. Of course not all mistakes concern amounts of flour. There is one which calls for 6 cups of butter (it should be 6 tablespoons) for a medium-size batch of dough. Another calls for ½ cup of ginger (should be ½ teaspoon) and finally a recipe which lists two amounts for shortening and none for sugar in a cake. Here one could only guess which is the amount to use for shortening and which for sugar. Thus a general knowledge of proportions between ingredients can eliminate most of the disappointments in baking.

Natural Unbleached Flour

At the request of their customers, more and more large supermarkets are stocking natural, unbleached flour. If it cannot be found in the flour section look for it on the shelves reserved for gourmet foods. When ordering natural flour from small mills there is sometimes a short waiting period as most of them grind only as orders are received so that the flour will be fresh when shipped. To keep it fresh in your home it should be stored in glass jars or plastic bags in refrigeratoi or freezer.

The three most appealing qualities of homemade bread—flavor, aroma and texture—can be most satisfactorily achieved by the use of natural flour. When freshly processed, the flour has a slight yellowish tint because of the small amount of carotin contained in the wheat. Natural oxidation lightens this tint in time. After one becomes used to baking with it, one can judge the freshness of the flour by its color when it is received.

Commercial bleaching was achieved by the addition of oxidizing gases or powder or by treating the flour with electrically produced nitrogen peroxide. Some presently used bleaching agents, along with other additives, increase the fermentation period of doughs and add to their toughness and stability, thus enabling the bakers to produce a satisfactory commercial bread from lower grade wheat.

Though there is slight probability that natural flour will ever again be used to produce commercially baked bread in quantity, more people are learning to use it every year with a great deal of pleasure. Since it packs more tightly than the presifted kind it is well to remember to sift it when substituting it in one of your favorite recipes until you learn what adjustments need to be made in proportions of flour to liquids.

When the wrappers of soft-whipped or twisted process loaves of much advertised brands of commercial bread are opened and one gets a whiff of the flat, pasty, unpleasant odor and then sees how the bread shrinks with loss of shape as it ages, it is apparent that the bread has been made with inferior flour. Dough which has been overworked will deteriorate quickly in the same way. It is very distressing to have a bite of bread become a gummy ball in one's mouth instead of breaking apart into tender crumbs, easy to swallow. The breads made with starter, especially those containing portions of the coarser, stone-ground flours and meals, all have tender crust and excellent crumb.

Basic Techniques

Baking Pans

Today there seem to be no regulations for pan sizes, so in this book I am classifying the sizes thus:

Miniature—4½ by 2½ by 1½ inches—½ cup dough
Small pans—7½ by 3½ by 2¼ inches—1½ cups dough
Medium pans—8½ by 4 by 2½ inches—2 cups dough
Large pans—9 by 5 by 2¾ inches—2½ cups dough.

The amounts of dough suggested for each pan will be just right to make loaves which will round up well above the rim of the pans for very light breads, and even with the rims for breads containing coarse meals or heavy with fruits and nuts.

Glass pans absorb heat quickly and the crust may be as brown as desired before the center of the bread is baked sufficiently. The thermostat should be set at least 25 degrees lower than the suggested temperature if it is 350°F. or more. Shiny metal pans reflect heat so that the crust will not brown as much as that of bread baked in a dull surfaced pan or one which has darkened from long use. When using Teflon-coated pans the crust will be darker on sides and bottom than on bread baked in uncoated metal pans at the same temperature.

Bread baked in glassware will have the thickest crust. There is very little difference, if any, in the thickness of the crust of loaves baked in dull surfaced or age darkened tin and Teflon-coated pans. The thinnest, most delicate crust is achieved by using light-weight aluminum pans.

Kneading Dough

If the inexperienced baker is hesitant about getting hands covered with sticky dough in learning to knead, there is a very simple way of avoiding this trouble. Spread the amount of flour reserved for the pastry board in a raised circle around a lightly floured center. Turn out dough into this ring. Go around the edge of the mound with a rubber plate scraper, turning it up so that the dough will be well floured all around. Then it is an easy matter to slip the fingers under far enough to lift and fold the dough, beginning to work in the flour. When this has been done one can really knead, turning the dough a little at a time as it is lifted, folded and pushed down with the palm of the hand until it forms a smooth nonsticky ball.

Some directions warn against over-kneading. I have yet to see any homemade bread which had been overworked. Vigorous kneading softens gluten in flour, making it more elastic and responsive to the leavening agent. However, poor texture can result from kneading in additional flour just before shaping dough for the pans. The gluten will not have time to ripen and that will result in tough, tight spots and, depending on the grade of flour used, will even cause discolored spots where it is not well distributed. Only enough flour should be used on the pastry board while molding or shaping the dough to keep it from sticking after it is cut into portions.

Testing Bread for Doneness

The accepted test is to lift pan and tap lightly on the bottom with fingers. If you are sensitive to heat, tap the pan with a wooden spoon or knife handle. If the bread is done it should emit a hollow sound. The pan should feel lighter than when placed in the oven. On plain breads the top crust should spring back when pushed lightly with the finger. Of course, this will not work with crusts which have been glazed to harden them during baking. Look to see if the bread has begun to shrink slightly from the sides of the pan. Do keep track of the time listed for the baking period but if you are not positive that your oven registers temperature correctly, watch carefully each time you try a new recipe so that you will be sure of how much time it takes to bake each kind of bread perfectly.

Remember, when using Teflon-coated utensils the side and bottom crusts of loaves and rolls baked in muffin pans will be darker than the top crusts. Don't just dump bread from the pan but remove it gently and, if you feel it is not baked quite as done as you like, carefully slip it back into the pan and return it to the oven for a short period.

No Stale Bread Please!

I dislike the term "stale bread" very much. To me it simply means bread which has been allowed to lose flavor and food value because of improper handling. When I read these words I always think of a picture in an old book about pioneers which showed a woman peeling the moldy crust from a huge round loaf as she stood by a covered wagon. There was real reason for having stale bread in those days but there is no excuse for it now. Yet we still read in modern cookbooks and magazines the terms "stale," "very stale," "the staler the better" and others. If the authors simply mean "dry bread" I think that is what they should write.

The majority of us have refrigerators or freezers or both now and there is even a simple way to keep bread fresh longer without either of these. (I do not like either plastic or metal boxes, particularly those which are fixed in cabinets, for many people do not wash and air them often enough.) The various methods for storing bread are described in the following sections.

Making Crumbs and Croutons

Rather than allow bread to become stale, why not use a portion of the baking to make, for freezing, sticks and croutons ready for toasting or sautéing, square or rounds for *croûtes*, and fresh or toasted crumbs for desserts, casseroles, crumb breads, etc. The trimmings from the sticks, squares and other shapes can be added to the crumb supply so that there is no waste. It is helpful to sift out fine crumbs and put up separately for use in breading meat, dusting baking pans, adding to any soups needing thickening so there is no need to sieve, etc. Package in double plastic sacks with label on the inner sack where it will not loosen or be rubbed off. Sometimes I process a whole baking except for one loaf or pan of rolls to use at once. This will, perhaps, make a six months supply with only a single washing of the grinder and clean up. This enables one to prepare certain dishes whenever desired even though there is no time for preliminary work. It doesn't take long to fill the jar with delicious Dutch Crumb Cookies (p. 169) when it only takes seconds to remove the package of crumbs from the freezer and slip off the rubber band. I try not to be without some white, rye, graham and spiced rusk crumbs in the freezer at all times.

Freezing Bread

I have never made a bread which did not freeze satisfactorily. Some breads, such as those containing fruit, nuts and spices improve in flavor from being frozen and I have kept some of these much longer than recommended on various freezing charts. It is not necessary to chill bread before slicing but one should have a good knife especially made for bread and use it for that purpose only. It is most convenient to slice all loaves before packaging unless they are to be used for some special purpose for which the unsliced is required. Wrap the bread as soon as it has cooled to retain the moisture needed to make it taste "fresh baked" when reheated. Bread will keep its shape better if the package is frozen on a flat surface before stacking in the freezer.

Bread can be packaged in meal-sized amounts (if anyone knows what the necessary amount will be when the time for that certain meal arrives) but it requires more time, and it is much harder to keep track of a large number of small packages in the freezer. There is no advantage in using slice dividers in the package for the slices can be readily separated by inserting a sharp pointed knife between them if this is done as soon as the bread is removed from the freezer and is still completely frozen.

Use only clear cellophane freezer wrap. (Two brands: Montgomery, Ward's "Tru-Cold" and Sears, Roebuck's "Coldspot" are available nationwide. Both come in 18″ by 100′ rolls and work equally well, although "Coldspot" is listed as a short time wrap.) Plastic wrap is unsatisfactory not only because it must be replaced with another wrapper before the bread can be reheated but also it is difficult to keep it from sticking together long enough to make straight top folds and neat, tight corners. It has been my experience when there was mechanical trouble with the freezer that the plastic-wrapped packages were the first on which the sealing tape loosened.

The magic transparent tape (Scotch brand, green label) which can be written on holds better and longer than the white freezer tape. (Occasionally the tape from a roll of the white variety doesn't hold well at all. I have been told that this defect is caused by the tape not being rolled onto the holder under the proper tension, thus allowing it to dry between the rounds.)

Aluminum foil is inconvenient to use because packages have to be opened to identify contents if a label becomes detached and this does occur sometimes, especially when the freezer is crowded. Foil, unless it is the heaviest grade which is hard to fold down tightly over soft bread, is very easily punctured even with a fingernail when it is cold. Again, the foil package must be opened if one wishes to check on the progress while the bread is being reheated.

In wrapping anything for the freezer the sheet of material should be wide enough to allow for a generous double fold the length of the package (called a "drug store wrap"), so there will be no possibility of the wrap gaping open even if the tape does not extend the full length of the closing. The ends of the wrapper should be long enough to make a full, mitred closing as deep as the height of the package, and the tape should come well down over the point of this closing. Rolls fit into freezer space more neatly when placed on flat disposable aluminum pans before wrapping, and coffee cakes are also more easily taken care of when they can be baked in disposable pans and left in them for freezing. These pans are sold almost everywhere.

Reheating Bread

Reheat bread in the cellophane freezer wrap. Do not reheat too far ahead of serving time. How much time to allow depends on whether the bread is completely thawed and also on the type of bread you are reheating. As a general rule, a dry type of bread, such as Babka, may be placed in a 300°F. oven with wrapper still sealed and partially thawed for about 45 minutes. A soft type, such as potato bread, will become too steamy if reheated without being completely thawed. A medium size loaf will take about 20 minutes to become warm throughout in a 300 degree oven. Hard–crusted bread should be completely thawed and heated quickly at 350 degrees with the wrapper opened at one end. Breads heavy with fruit and nuts are best when warmed slowly at very low heat. If they have been thawed completely heat with wrapper sealed; if they are still frozen and contain a large amount of moisture the wrapper may be opened slightly at one end.

Bread Storage in Refrigerator

Bread should be completely cold before it is wrapped. Put it in a plastic bag and store it in the refrigerator, all through the

year. If there is no space in the refrigerator you can use the
bread box.

Bread Storage in Bread Box

Be sure the box is thoroughly cleaned and dried before fresh
bread is placed in it. If moisture is a problem, wrap completely
cooled bread in a double thickness of paper towels, then slip it
into a plastic bag, leaving the end open. Change towels daily.
The toweling absorbs moisture; when the bag is used without the
toweling, moisture collects on the plastic and drops back onto
the bread, making damp spots which will quickly cause mold.

Treatment of Crusts

Softening mediums: There are many ways to change the appearance and taste of crusts. Everyone, I am sure, is familiar
with brushing crusts after bread is baked with fats such as butter, margarine, oil, lard, etc., to keep crust soft. These softeners
should not be used if the crust is to be sprinkled with seeds such
as sesame or poppy, crumbs, or finely chopped nuts which are
expected to cling firmly.

When breads are to be sprinkled with seeds or nuts: Coat the
tops of these doughs with flour or place them before rising in a
large plastic bag, supported so that it will not touch dough while
it is rising. This prevents the top from drying. When ready for
the oven, the top of the dough can then be brushed with water,
wine or milk or with 1 egg white beaten with 1 tablespoon water
before sprinkling with seeds or other topping.

More About Crusts

All hard-crusted breads benefit by the use of steam in the
oven. A 9-inch layer-cake pan three-fourths full of water will pro-

vide a sufficient amount of steam. It should be put on the floor of the oven when the heat is turned on; if it is put in when the bread is, hot water should be used if the steam is needed during the first part of the baking period. Commercial baking directions call for removing the water during the last half of the baking period for some types of bread in some recipe books but others do not mention it so evidently there is no hard and fast rule about this matter.

Crust lovers who care to take time for the ultimate treatment for crust can do this: bake the bread in glass pans if possible and when done, remove from pan onto waxed paper, brush all over (top, sides and bottom) with heavy cream or undiluted canned milk. Place on lightly greased cooling rack and set in the oven for about 5 minutes. If the crust is not too brown turn the heat up slightly for these few minutes.

Finishing Touches

For a rich, shiny glaze nothing is better than undiluted canned milk brushed on twice, the first time either before placing bread in oven or halfway through the baking period and again about 5 minutes before removing from the oven. This gives a lovely russet color. Brushing twice with an egg yolk beaten with 1 teaspoon of milk also gives a nice shiny glaze but the brown is more yellowish. French or Italian-style loaves may be brushed with a glaze made by cooking together 1½ teaspoons cornstarch, ½ teaspoon salt and ½ cup water. Cool before applying. A glaze for Leopard or Tiger crust is made by preparing the following: about 10 minutes before loaves are ready for oven, stir ½ teaspoon dry yeast and 1 teaspoon sugar into 2 tablespoons warm water. When it foams stir in 2 tablespoons cornstarch or arrowroot and 1 teaspoon oil. When bread is ready for the oven stir this well and brush thickly over loaf.

For a sweet finish combine 1 cup confectioners sugar with 2 tablespoons liquid and a few drops of flavoring as desired. White wine makes the clearest glaze and eliminates the rather raw taste that this glaze sometimes has, but milk or fruit juice may be used. Pour over bread when it has partially cooled after being removed from oven.

How to Add Variety to Your Baking

Here is a direct quote from *New System of Bread Making*: "Do not too slavishly adhere to all the rules and dictums laid down in this or any other trade book, for the instructions given may not exactly fit every individual case. You have a mind of your own and have been endowed with intellectual faculties. *Why not use them?*" I echo this author's advice for how else are we to learn new methods and different pleasing combinations of ingredients? The basic recipe is just that—basic—a foundation to launch your experiments from. As soon as you are familiar with a recipe from the method of mixing to the finished product, then you are ready to start adapting it to your own tastes.

Vary the Texture

For a crisper, crunchier bread, try potato flour or potato starch. Start out by using 1 cupful in a recipe which calls for about 8 cups of white flour, then substitute more in succeeding batches until you find how much gives you the results most pleasing to you.

For a finer textured, more solid bread, try reducing the amount of yeast, a little each time, and allowing a longer period for rising until you have the right amount to give the results you like best. For coarser, lighter texture, use more leavening for quicker rising, and substitute meals of various kinds such as sunflower seed, pumpkin seed, coconut, dark rye, etc., for about one-quarter the amount of flour called for.

For a flakier crust and more tender crumb, substitute egg yolks for a part of the liquid (about 3 yolks for ½ cup).

Vary Herbs and Spices

Change the combination of herbs in the recipe. Think of all those available: basil, marjoram, tarragon, thyme, rosemary, dill weed, chervil, sage plus the aromatic seeds which emit such teasing aroma during the baking periods such as celery, fennel, caraway, anise, dill and cumin.

Do the same with spices. With all of these things do not use too large an amount the first time. The merest whisper of a different taste or smell is far preferable to a heavy accent. Just one-half teaspoon of white pepper added to a four-loaf batch of white bread can give a piquant, tantalizing hint of flavor which makes one want to eat more to find out what it really is. A tiny sprinkle of allspice for plain cinnamon rolls adds that extra something which always makes people ask for the recipe.

Add Fruits and Nuts

Don't forget the flavor lift which the different kinds of raisins, currants, dried fruits such as pears, apples, peaches and prunes, and candied fruits can add to any plain bread.

Add 1 cup of lightly toasted coconut, or nuts of any kind, which has been put through a *mouli* grater, to any white or egg bread (a three- to four-loaf batch) for a richer, more distinctive flavor, especially when making coffee rounds, sweet rolls, crescents, etc.

Vary the Liquid

Fresh milk, scalded and cooled, may be used instead of water in most recipes, or ½ canned, evaporated milk and ½ water for fresh milk, or an equal amount of dried instant whey, or dried buttermilk for dried skim milk, etc. Instant whey is particularly good to use for it seems to have equal or, perhaps even greater, value than potatoes as a yeast booster because of certain enzymes it contains. Just as my mother did for so long, I always saved a portion of fresh whey from the cottage cheese to make bread when we had milk cows.

When using 1 cup of wheat germ (the brand which is sweetened and toasted gives the best flavor) substitute unsweetened apple, prune, fig or apricot juice for the liquid in the basic recipe. If sweetened juice must be used, omit part or all of the sweetener called for in the original list of ingredients.

For herb breads, substitute meat broths for liquid. Broth from stewed chicken gives a delicate yellow tint to white bread. Beef broth from pot roast cooked with wine and juniper berries is marvelous in bread to be used for lettuce and tomato or egg salad sandwiches.

Fats

Just about the softest, most delicate-textured bread possible is made with chicken fat for shortening. Beef fat is fine for bread to be used hot but makes the bread quite hard when cold. It can be used to best advantage when making hamburger buns to be served piping hot.

Health Food Additions

I am not a health food faddist but I do admit to being addicted to delicious flavors and appetizing aromas, so if any health food products will help to achieve these results in baking,

I am willing to use any I can secure. If better health comes from their use it is a truly welcome bonus.

I have tried most of the unusual but edible ingredients mentioned in the old books that I have been able to find in this country, with the exception of lily bulbs, iris rhizomes and ragwort roots. I am deterred from using the first two because of the thought of all the lovely future flowers I would be destroying. As for the ragwort, it just does not appeal to me, although bread made with it was said to be easily digested, more nutritive and "exhilarating" than wheat bread and to have an agreeable, nut-like flavor.

The authority for this information also mentioned that it was said the same properties could be found in radishes but he doubted it. I do not know why the huge white radishes sold in the markets in Germany would not make as good a bread as turnips or parsnips. I intend to try them if I can ever raise any to a good size and keep them sweet and crisp.

Several kinds of beans, every kind of cereal available, turnips, parsnips, pumpkin, squash, sweet potatoes and chestnuts have all proved valuable for providing variety in baking. Fermented dried green peas were used in one ancient Persian recipe which I found recorded in a rare old book printed in London in 1695. The ferment was lively and the resulting bread was light and baked nicely, but only my flock of Ancona laying hens shared the Persians' appreciation for this loaf. They ate every crumb with relish after my family refused the bread completely because of its peculiar yellowish-green shade and a very unpleasant odor reminiscent of green hay which had lain wet too long. On the other hand, the color made no difference when I tried an old Russian peasant recipe for a rye bread using syrup from crab-apple pickles for the liquid. It had a most unattractive, rusty tint, but the flavor was very piquant and the crust as crunchy as anyone could wish.

When a friend mentioned in her cookery column in our city newspaper that I was using peach leaves for making homemade yeast, she was deluged with mail from people asking if I was not using a poisonous product. The state horticultural agent was contacted and he gave this statement in his column, ". . . as used in making yeast by the old recipe, there is no probability of harm. Most of the members of the *Prunus* group do contain hydrocyanic acid (this is the same as found in the manioc root from which tapioca is made). Wild cherries and wild plums have proven fatal to livestock eating the wilted leaves. Peaches do not appear to have a problem in this sense . . ."

If it had been poisonous I would never have gotten the recipe. The woman who gave it to me was seventy-six years old at the time and liked to boast that she had never been sick a day in her life until she was past seventy-five. She was raised in Oklahoma Territory with a houseful of brothers and sisters. When she was old enough, it became her duty to take care of the peach leaf yeast while it was drying, turning and stirring it several times a day. Her mother did not bother to make it into cakes but crumbled it into small particles as it dried to complete the process more quickly. When it was thoroughly dry it was stored in muslin sacks hung in the attic. On baking days it was measured out by the handfuls according to the size of the batch of dough being mixed.

Visit your health food shops or order by mail (I give a list of sources later in this book) for ingredients to give variety. Try both brown and white rice flour, oat flour, ground millet, combinations of cracked grains, different vegetable and seed oils, flavorings, etc. I saved rose petals for a fragrance jar with no thought at the time that they would be used for anything else, but later I crushed and stirred them into some bread dough with delightful results.

Use the sweetening agent which appeals to you. If you like

a bread which tastes completely unsweetened use white corn syrup or glucose, which is hard to find but worth looking for. If for reasons of health no natural sweetening can be used, substitute artificial products according to directions for amounts on the container.

Bread Forms

It is safe to say that if one could bake only a single basic bread, variety in shaping and crust treatment would allow the serving of a different-looking bread at every meal for a month without straining the baker's ability. This is one of the greatest pleasures of home baking. Here are just a few of the favorite forms, starting with the traditional ways of shaping the plain loaf.

Well-Rounded Loaf—Flatten the loaf-size portion of dough into an oval three times the width of the pan. Fold one rounded end over the center and the other end over that. Place in a pan seam-side down. Thus the center of the loaf will be higher than the ends when baked.

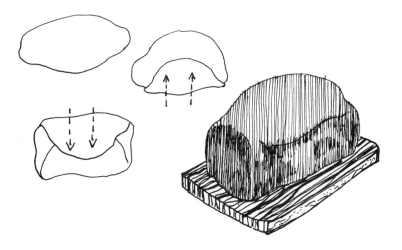

Rolled Loaf—Flatten loaf-size portion of dough into long rectangle as wide as the length of the pan. Roll up evenly and place seam-side down in pan with ends flat against the pan, not turned under. This gives uniform height the length of the loaf which makes it especially nice for sandwiches.

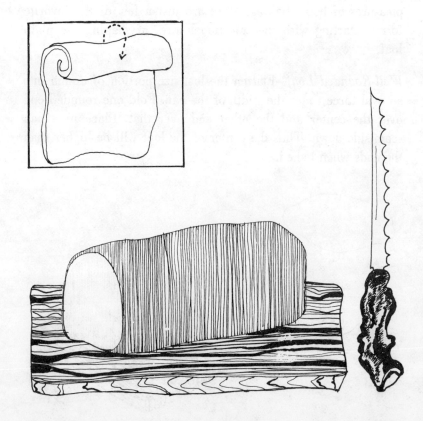

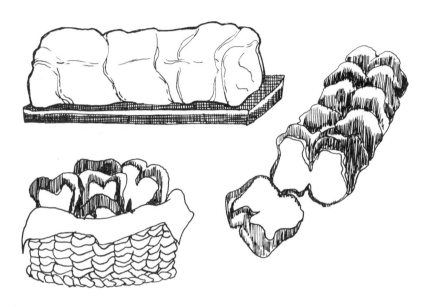

Long Twist Loaf—Divide loaf-size portion in half. Roll each piece with hands into a strand about one half again as long as pan. Twist together with as many turns as possible and place in pan with ends flat against pan, not turned over. This is said to improve the texture of the bread.

Pull-apart Loaf—Divide loaf-size portion of dough into an even number of small roll-size pieces. Shape into smooth balls, coat with melted butter, then press tightly together in loaf pan, a single row for small pan and a double row for large pan. When risen, each section will be about the thickness of a slice. These loaves should be served warm and the sections pulled apart with a fork. For special occasions, pull apart, spread on flat pan and toast quickly under broiler. Pile in wicker basket lined with napkin.

Wrapped Loaf—When adding fruit and nuts to just a few of the loaves from a batch of bread, if you do not care for the dried pieces in the baked crust, reserve a small portion of plain dough. Flatten into thin rectangle and wrap around the fruit-filled loaf.

Two-Tone Loaf—When making up two kinds of dough at the same time, such as graham or rye and white, wrap a thin sheet of one dough around the shaped loaf of the other.

Marble Loaf—Using two strands each of two different kinds of dough, about one half again as long as loaf pan to be used, lay two on top of the others checkerboard fashion, then twist. Place in pan with ends flat against pan, not turned under.

Cottage Loaf—A stiffer dough should be used for this shape but regular dough can be used by baking loaf in a round pan about 2½ inches high instead of on a flat surface. Divide loaf-size portion of dough into two pieces, with one for the base about one-half again as large as the other. Shape larger piece into ball, place in pan and flatten so that it is level across the top. Shape smaller piece the same way but flatten on bottom and place on center of base. Either brush with butter or sprinkle flour heavily over surface. Let rise about half, then press center of top gently down against base. Let rise until quite light before baking. If flour coating is used, brush away excess with pastry brush after removing from pan.

Notched Cottage Loaf—Proceed as for plain Cottage Loaf. When dough is ready for oven, if baking in pan, cut slits evenly around sides of top section with sharp scissors. If baking on flat surface, cut matching slits on sides of bottom section also.

Coiled Loaf—Shape loaf-size portion of dough into rectangle about twice the length of diameter of round pan to be used and about 5 inches wide. Fold in half lengthwise. Roll up and place with open side of fold down. Pinch end to fasten so that roll will not uncoil. Brush generously with butter so that ridges will remain separated.

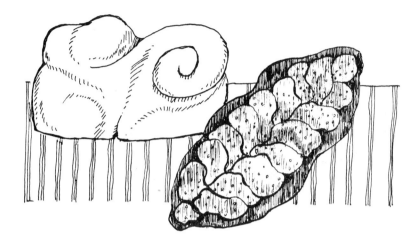

S-Scroll Loaf—Prepare dough as for Coiled Loaf with the folded strips at least twice as long as loaf pan to be used. Roll one end of strip to center, turn over and roll the other end to center in opposite direction. Lift carefully and place in loaf pan with open side of fold down. Brush generously with butter so that ridges will remain separated as they rise.

English Challah—Divide a loaf-size portion of dough into two pieces with one being about twice as large as the other. Shape larger piece into elongated boat shape with tapered ends. Divide smaller piece into thirds. Shape into slender strands and braid. It should be as long as the boat-shaped base. Brush the center of this with water and place braid on top. For a hard-crusted bread, slip pan into large plastic bag, supported so that it will not touch dough, until loaf is light. Brush with cold water before placing in oven and bake with pan of boiling water on floor of **oven.**

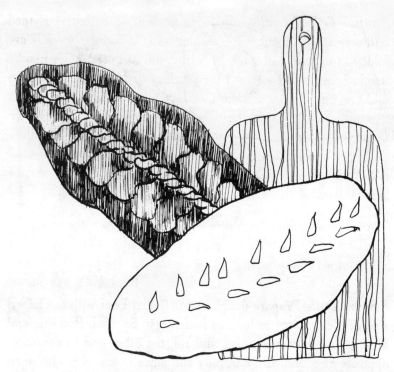

Dutch Challah—Proceed as for English Challah except that a small piece of dough is reserved before dividing into the two sections to make a pencil-size rope to lay along center of top braid. A small lengthwise cut in braid is made to lay strand in to prevent it from slipping as dough rises.

Dutch Scissor Loaf—Shape loaf-size portion of stiff dough into a long oval shape. Place on flat pan. Brush with butter or dust heavily with flour. Let rise about half. Snip an alternate line of incisions with sharp scissors along each side of the center. For hard crust, bake loaf with floured surface with pan of boiling water on floor of oven. Brush crust with cold water or white wine a few minutes before end of baking period.

Scottish French Loaf—A loaf-size portion of dough is shaped into a rectangle about twice as long as it is wide. The ends are folded in to meet in center. A rolling pin or broad knife handle should be pressed hard over the joining. Brush with butter, then fold one half over top. Brush surface all over with butter. Let rise until very light. If the dough is quite soft the loaf can be supported against one side of a square pan which is wider than the loaf. This odd shape was known in some areas as the "piano" loaf. It gives a large amount of delicious crust for the size of the loaf.

Baton Loaves—These come in many shapes from the short fat English Bloomer to the long slim French and Italian loaves with many top cut patterns and crust treatments. I suppose even salt sticks could be classified as miniature batons. Most are baked with steam. Some bakers remove pan of water for the second half of baking period.

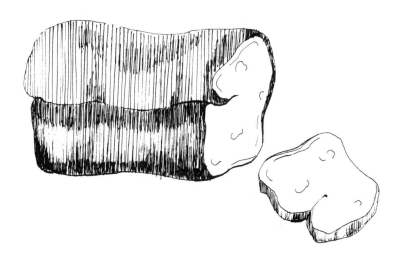

English Bloomer—This loaf is shaped into a roll about 12 inches long, 4 inches wide and about as high. When light it is cut along the top in either a herringbone or scroll design. This is baked on flat surface with steam for only the first 5 to 10 minutes of the baking period.

Belgian Baton—This loaf is only about 9 inches long with four or five diagonal cuts the width of the top.

Leopard Baton—A long loaf with square ends, no cuts on top and brushed with a thick coating of paste made from white flour, rice flour, sugar and oil or a yeast paste just before placing in the oven. The crust is crisp and crunchy with spotted, crackled surface.

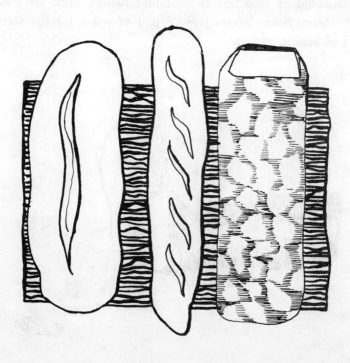

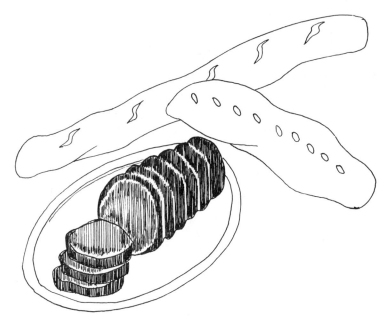

French Long Loaf—These are from 18 to 36 inches long and, in France, are made from a softer dough so that they are usually baked in cloth-lined baskets or perforated wire trays. They are brushed with a mixture of milk and water before cutting top and baking.

Italian Long Loaf—These are made in same shape as the French but are not so long. The dough is enriched with milk, sugar, fat and eggs. The cuts on top are much closer together and shorter than those on the French loaf.

Musket Loaf—These were also called "toast" loaves and baked in the round by using hinged, fluted pans. We can make half-rounds in the fluted nut bread pans available to us. The slices are beautiful because of their rounded edges and they can be cut evenly by following the fluting creases.

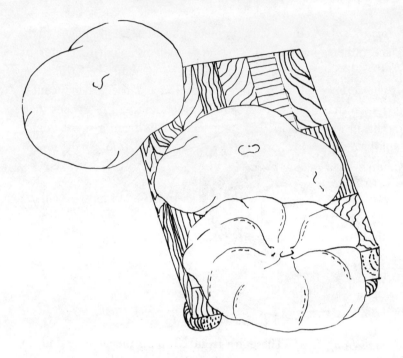

Flat Loaf—In England these were called Devon Flats. About 1½ cups of rich bread dough were rolled to an 8-inch circle and placed on flat pan. When very light, a deep indentation was made in the center of the circle before placing in oven. In the Scandinavian countries the rounds were made from dough containing mostly coarse rye meal. A small circle was made in the center and sometimes, just before baking, slits like rows of stitching were made with the point of a sharp knife to mark the round into wedges. These flat loaves were baked in large numbers until very dry and hard, then strung on a round stick like a broom handle and hung from the ceiling. It is nice to make these flat loaves for smorgasbords.

Crown Loaf—Using a large, round pan at least 3 inches high, place either four balls or one large ball of dough in center of pan. Roll out three strands of dough each about 1½ times the circumference of pan. Braid them. Place close around center dough so that it cannot spread too much and will be higher than the braid when baked. This is usually made from a sweet dough and decorated with icing and "jewels" made from bits of bright candied fruit when the loaf has cooled.

Large Brioche-shaped Loaf—Into a fluted mold put a ball of dough large enough to fill it to within about 1 inch of the top, so that the bread will puff up high above the rim when baked. Make a hollow in center of ball with three fingers pressed down firmly. Insert small ball of dough which has been pinched to a point at the bottom into this opening. Let rise until very light and brush with beaten egg yolk and water before placing in oven and again shortly before end of baking period, if desired.

As for roll shapes there can be no end to the variety as long as there are people who enjoy working with dough as a sculptor works with clay. Here are a few of the shapes we discovered in the baskets of breakfast breads served in Europe.

Kaiser Roll—Flatten muffin-size balls of dough into circles 3 to
3½ inches across. Place thumb of left hand a little to left of
center of a circle and keep it in this position until last fold is
made. With right hand lift edge of circle, bring it up over thumb
and press firmly into center. Press down fold from center to
edge with side of hand. Continue on around, lifting edge of circle
at equal distances, bringing it up over and pressing down in center until the fifth time when the point of fold is tucked into the
hole made by left thumb. This makes a whirligig pattern on top
of roll. They will retain their shape better if kept fairly cool,
about 70 degrees, while rising. Bake with pan of boiling water
on floor of oven. Brush with water or combination of egg white
and water just before placing in oven and again just before end
of baking period. There is a modern shortcut for making these
rolls, a Kaiser roll cutter with four curved blades set on a flat
disc with which one cuts the whirligig design when rolls are
partially risen.

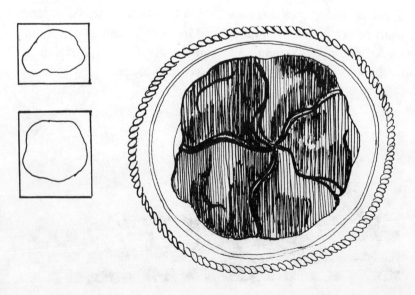

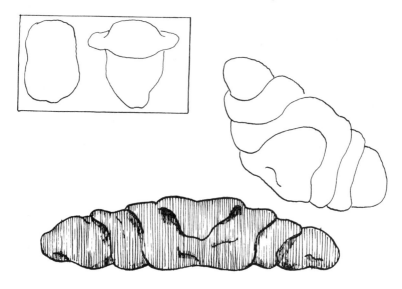

Viennese Roll—Flatten muffin-size balls of dough into fairly thin circles about as wide as the length desired for rolls. Let stand a few minutes covered with a light cloth. Fold over curve of circle at far side and stretch under part slightly. Stretch the near side of circle into elongated triangle with blunt end. Roll and stretch as you roll, ending with tip or "lip" facing upwards. Brush with milk or water under this tip and press down with rolling pin. Set to rise and bake the same as for Kaiser Rolls.

Continental Baton—This is shaped the same as the Viennese except that it is stretched longer as it is rolled and thus made much thinner so that it is nearly all crust.

Short Vienna Rolls—Make small pointed boat shapes about 4 inches long. After brushing surface with water just before placing in oven, make 2 diagonal "leaf" cuts on top. There is a special knife for doing this in bakeries but it can be done very nicely with sharp, pointed scissors or razor blade held at a 45 degree angle to the surface. The slanting of the cut is what makes it spread open to look very much like a leaf with one edge slightly rolled.

Italianii Roll—Shape dough by constricting center of ball until it is almost divided. Flatten each side into a long oval connected by narrow center strip to look somewhat like a dumbbell. Let rest for a few minutes covered with a light cloth. Stretch ends slightly if necessary to make them the same size. Roll both to the center. Place on pan with connecting strip up. Just before placing in oven snip the strip so that rolls can expand.

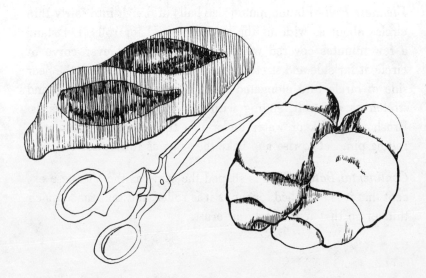

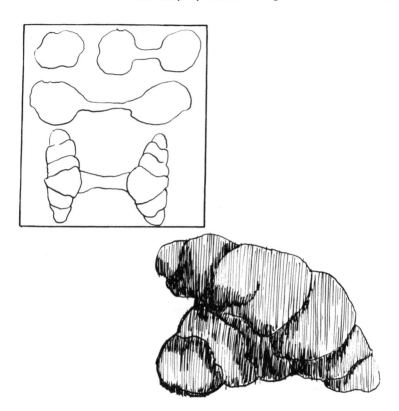

Cannon Roll—Shape the same as for the Italianii but place on pan with connecting strip down. Twist one roll around and up over the center of the other one with the top one not quite centered over the lower one so that the end will point up like a cannon ready to be fired.

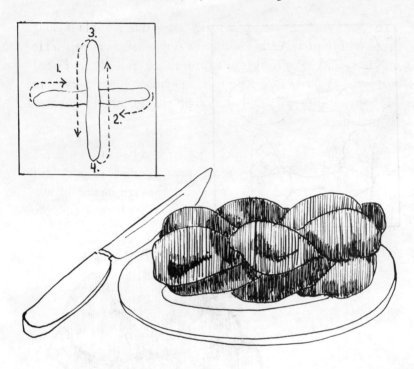

Plaited Roll—Cut each roll-size portion of dough in half. Roll each into a rope about 7 inches long. Lay one over the other to form a cross. Press in the middle to stick them together. Take two opposite ends and cross over first two. Take other two ends and cross them over. Continue braiding upwards from table until length is used up. Press ends together. Lay on side on lightly greased baking sheet. When ready for oven brush with whole beaten egg.

The following shapes are equally attractive for plain dough spread with butter before rolling, or for sweet dough sprinkled with sugar and spice or spread with fruit and nut filling. For all, the dough is rolled into a long rectangle about ⅓-inch thick and wide enough so that it will be the right size for muffin tins when cut into slices.

Butterfly Roll—Cut double thick slice from roll. Place on pan in same upright position as when cut. Press rounded edge of knife handle or small round stick downward through center of slice until it touches the pan and inner edge of both coils come together in center.

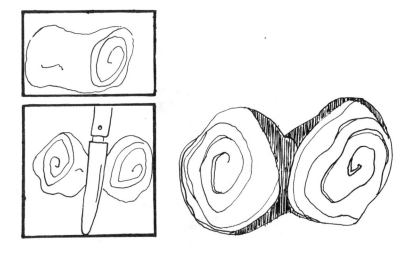

Spectacle Roll—Cut double slice of roll almost through in center. Open out flat with connecting strip of dough up.

Fan Roll—Cut three thin slices of roll almost through to bottom. Lay on pan and spread out in arc with each slice just overlapping the edge of the one before it.

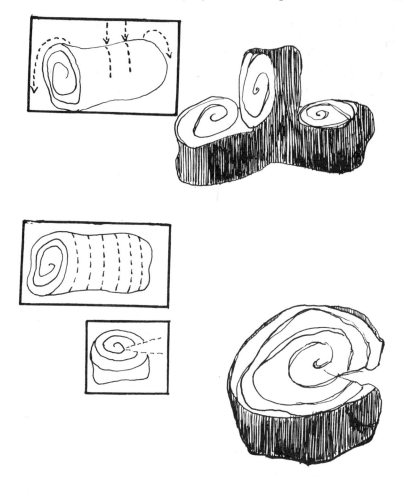

Basket Roll—Cut three slices almost through to bottom, with the center slice a little thinner than the others. Place on pan with 2 outside slices laid flat and the center one left standing.

Arc Roll—Lay cut slices flat on pan. Cut with sharp knife from edge at lap to center. Spread from cut to form arc and separate slightly at the ends.

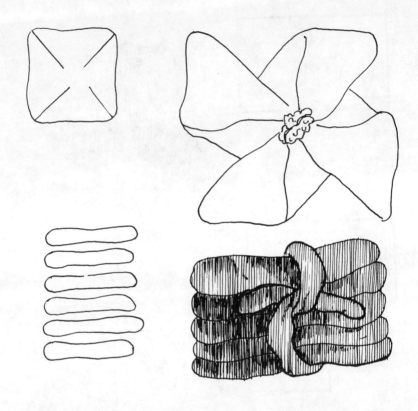

Now for a few very quickly made rolls which hardly take any more time than filling a pan with plain buns.

Whirligig Roll—Cut ⅓-inch-thick rectangle of dough into 4-inch squares. Cut almost to center from each corner. Lift every other point, fold over to center and press down. Leave plain or place a nut half or spoonful of jam in center.

Bundle of Sticks Roll—Divide each roll-size portion of dough into 6 equal pieces. Shape into little rolls about 3½ inches long. Coat with butter by rolling from end to end of generously buttered pan. Lay 5 sticks together crosswise on top of 6th stick. Stretch each end of this long enough to bring up and twist together on top.

Bow Tie Roll—Cut 2x4-inch rectangles of ⅓-inch-thick dough. Twist in the center and press down to hold. If desired, glaze surface with egg and decorate with design in bright candy toppings.

Pyramid Roll—Cut ½-inch-thick dough into 1½, 2 and 2½-inch circles. Place larger ones on pan and center others on top in order, brushing with milk or water between layers to keep in place. If rolls are to be left plain, make tiny balls of dough and place in dent made with finger in center top. If they are sweet rolls decorate after baking with a candied cherry or small marzipan fruit on top and dribble whatever kind of icing is desired down over the sides.

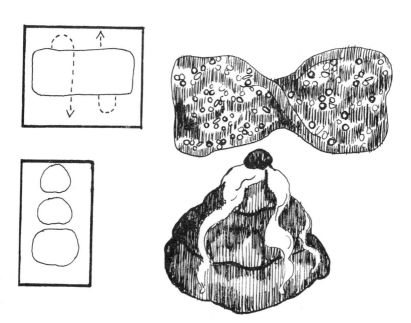

Open 8 Roll—Make a roll-size portion of dough into a rope about 7 or 8 inches long. With ends even, twist at the middle to make the upper loop for a figure 8. Leave the two ends straight. The Italians press a slice of hard-boiled egg into the center of the twist. I prefer a large English walnut or pecan half.

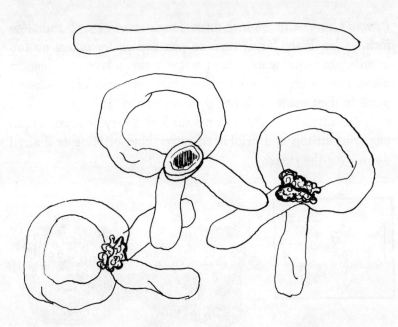

3

Grated Raw Potato Starter and 51 Recipes

Grated Raw Potato Starter

1 cup warm water
1½ cups white flour
1 teaspoon salt

1 teaspoon sugar
1 grated raw potato,
  medium size

Mix the 1 cup warm water, 1½ cups white flour and 1 teaspoon each salt and sugar in a 2-cup measure. Add enough grated potato to make 2 cups. Place in a wide-mouth glass jar or small mixing bowl (do not use metal or plastic) which will hold about 1 quart. Cover with a single thickness of cheesecloth to allow wild yeast from the air to settle into it for 24 hours. Stir well, cover tightly with a clinging transparent wrap which will cause the moisture to drip back and keep top of mixture from drying. Stir several times a day. In two or three days it will become foamy and very light. (The length of time depends on the temperature. 80-85°F. is ideal. It can go a little below 80° without harm, only slowing the procedure a little, but if it goes much higher than 85° it will be spoiled.)

Then stir well, pour into glass jar with screw-top lid and store in refrigerator at about 38 degrees. As soon as ½ inch of clear liquid has risen to the top it has ripened enough to start using. Do not be concerned if the mixture turns dark because of the raw potato during the fermentation period. It does not affect the bread made from it in any way and, as soon as the starter is mature, it will become a snowy white.

To renew starter: Add 1½ cups white flour and 1½ cups water each time it is used so that there are always 2 cups to bake with and 2 full cups to return to refrigerator. If for some reason it cannot be used regularly about twice a week, add 1 teaspoon sugar and stir well every three or four days.

Basic Starter Bread

2 cups starter	2 cups warm water
1½ cups cold water	1 cup dried skim milk powder
1½ cups white flour	4 tablespoons sugar
	3 cups white flour
½ cup warm water	4 tablespoons soft lard
1 teaspoon sugar	3 teaspoons salt
½ teaspoon ginger	4½ cups white flour
1 package dry yeast	

Empty starter from glass jar into large mixing bowl (do not use metal or plastic). Add 1½ cups cold water and 1½ cups white flour. Beat thoroughly. Cover tightly (clinging transparent wrap is good) and set in warm place (about 80°F.) overnight. Wash and scald starter jar and lid. Allow to air out overnight.

In the morning stir the starter thoroughly. Pour off 2 cups and set aside. Pour remaining 2 cups into glass jar, cover and return to refrigerator. Mix the ½ cup warm water, 1 teaspoon sugar, ½ teaspoon ginger and 1 package dry yeast. Set in warm place until foaming nicely. Pour the 2 cups reserved starter into mixing bowl. Add 2 cups warm water, 1 cup dry milk, 4 tablespoons sugar and 3 cups white flour. Beat thoroughly. Add the dry yeast mixture as soon as ready and beat again. Add 4 tablespoons soft lard, 3 teaspoons salt and 3½ cups white flour. Stir until the dough clears the bowl. Spread remaining 1 cup white flour on the pastry board. Turn out dough and knead thoroughly using a little more flour if necessary to make a smooth nonsticky dough. Return to bowl, grease top of dough, cover and set in warm place to rise until about double in bulk or until dent remains when pushed with finger, which should take about 1 hour at 80 to 85 degrees.

Turn out dough. Knead thoroughly without using any more flour than necessary. Divide and shape as desired. Place in well greased pans. Brush tops of dough with lard or butter, or if desired, roll top of loaf in thick layer of flour before placing in pan. Cover with light cloth and set in warm place to rise until dent remains in dough when pushed down lightly with finger. Bake in oven preheated to 375 degrees about 45 minutes for medium-size loaves. This recipe makes 4 loaves which will round up well above the top of the pan if allowed to rise almost to the rim before placing in the oven. A 1-loaf portion of the dough will make 1 9x9-inch pan of dinner rolls or 12 cinnamon or butter-flake rolls in large muffin tins.

To make an attractive bread to accompany a crisp vegetable salad, take a 1-loaf portion of the dough and roll out into a rectangle with the width equal to the length of the loaf pan. Spread with soft butter. Sprinkle lightly with coarse red and black seasoned pepper and celery seed. Roll up and seal. If available, lay a row of fresh sage leaves in the bottom of the buttered pan before putting in the loaf, seam-side down. Decorate top with more sage leaves and brush soft butter over surface of dough around them. Bake according to directions for plain bread.

Carob Nut Bread

2 cups starter
1½ cups cold water
1½ cups white flour

½ cup warm water
1 teaspoon sugar
½ teaspoon ginger
1 package dry yeast
1 cup milk, scalded and
　cooled

4 tablespoons sugar
6 tablespoons carob powder*
1 cup white flour
2 teaspoons vanilla
1 teaspoon salt
2 tablespoons soft butter
1 cup (or more) coarsely
　chopped English walnuts
3½ cups white flour

In the evening, empty starter from glass jar into large mixing bowl (do not use metal or plastic). Add 1½ cups cold water and 1½ cups white flour. Beat thoroughly. Cover tightly (clinging transparent wrap is good) and set in warm place (about 80°F.) overnight. Wash and scald starter jar and lid. Allow to air out overnight.

In the morning stir the starter thoroughly. Pour off 2 cups and set aside. Pour the remaining 2 cups into glass jar, cover and return to refrigerator. Mix the ½ cup warm water, 1 teaspoon sugar, ½ teaspoon ginger and 1 package dry yeast. Let set in warm place until foaming nicely. Pour the 2 cups reserved starter into mixing bowl. Add 1 cup cooled milk, 4 tablespoons sugar, 6 tablespoons carob powder and 1 cup white flour. Mix well. Add the dry yeast mixture as soon as ready. Beat well. Add 2 teaspoons vanilla, 1 teaspoon salt, 2 teaspoons soft butter and the 1 cup walnuts stirred into the 2½ cups white flour. Stir until the dough clears the bowl.

Spread the remaining 1 cup white flour on the pastry board.

---

* See Sources of Supply.

Turn out dough and knead well using a little more flour if necessary to make a smooth nonsticky dough. Return to bowl, brush top of dough with butter, cover and let rise in warm place until light. Turn out dough, knead, divide and shape as desired. Place in buttered pans, brush tops with butter and let set in warm place until light. Bake in oven preheated to 375 degrees for about 45 minutes. This recipe makes 4 high, well-rounded small loaves.

This bread makes wonderful toast and it is most attractive for sandwiches with cream cheese filling when baked in the large-size tin fruit cans. It is a very versatile bread for dieters as one or more of the ingredients can be omitted or substituted for without greatly affecting taste or texture, such as the salt or the sugar. Cocoa may be used in place of the carob powder, which is sweet and chocolaty, but it is not as good. The nuts may be omitted from the dough, then ground and mixed with sweetened condensed milk and flavoring to use as a topping for a pan of small buns or a coffee round made from a 1-loaf portion of the dough.

Toasted Corn Meal Bread

2 cups starter
1½ cups cold water
1½ cups white flour

½ cup warm water
1 teaspoon sugar
½ teaspoon ginger
1 package dry yeast
2 cups warm water

1 cup dried skim milk powder
4 tablespoons maple flavored syrup
3 cups white flour
3 cups toasted corn meal
3 teaspoons salt
4 tablespoons soft butter
2½ cups white flour

Empty starter from glass jar into large mixing bowl (do not use metal or plastic). Add 1½ cups cold water and 1½ cups white flour. Beat thoroughly. Cover tightly (clinging transparent wrap is good) and set in warm place (about 80°F.) overnight. Wash and scald starter jar and lid. Allow to air out overnight.

In the morning stir the starter thoroughly. Pour off 2 cups and set aside. Pour remaining 2 cups into glass jar, cover and return to refrigerator. Mix the ½ cup warm water, 1 teaspoon sugar, ½ teaspoon ginger and 1 package dry yeast. Set in warm place until foaming nicely. Pour the 2 cups reserved starter into mixing bowl. Add 2 cups warm water, 1 cup dried milk, 4 tablespoons syrup, 3 cups white flour and 3 cups corn meal. Beat thoroughly. Add the dry yeast mixture as soon as ready and beat again. Add 3 teaspoons salt, 4 tablespoons soft butter and 1½ cups white flour. Stir until the dough clears the bowl.

Spread remaining 1 cup white flour on pastry board. Turn out dough and knead well, using only as much flour as necessary to make a smooth, nonsticky dough. Return to bowl, grease top of dough, cover and set in warm place until light. Turn out, knead well, divide and shape into loaves. Place in greased pans, brush tops with butter, cover with cloth and set in warm place until light. Bake in oven preheated to 375 degrees for 45 to 50 minutes. If crust is not as brown as desired, turn oven up to 425 degrees for about 5 minutes at end of baking period. This will make 4 high, rather flat-topped medium loaves.

A 1-loaf portion of dough will make 12 large crusty butter rolls. Roll portion of dough into rectangle, brush generously with butter, roll up from long side, cut into 1 to 1½-inch slices and place cut-side down in buttered muffin tins. When light bake at 375 degrees for about 25 minutes.

Use this bread for one-half the amount called for in your

favorite dressing recipe for a delicious accompaniment to any roast fowl or meat, or use it in place of the Hickory Smoked Corn Bread called for in the recipe for Chestnut Dressing Supreme (p. 162).

Note: If ready-toasted corn meal is unavailable, place 3 cups finest yellow corn meal (white meal may be used but the color of the bread will not be as attractive) in oven at 350 degrees and toast until lightly browned. Watch carefully and stir often. Prepare this and cool before starting to mix dough. A quantity can be prepared at one time and stored in a moisture-proof container in the freezer.

Buckwheat Bread

2 cups starter	1 cup scalded and cooled
1½ cups cold water	milk
1½ cups white flour	4 tablespoons brown sugar or
	sorghum
½ cup warm water	2 cups buckwheat flour
1 teaspoon sugar	4 tablespoons soft butter
½ teaspoon ginger	1½ teaspoons salt
1 package dry yeast	4 cups white flour

Empty starter from glass jar into large mixing bowl (do not use metal or plastic). Add 1½ cups cold water and 1½ cups white flour. Beat thoroughly. Cover tightly (clinging transparent wrap is good) and set in warm place (about 80°F.) overnight. Wash and scald starter jar and lid. Allow to air out overnight.

In the morning stir the starter thoroughly. Pour off 2 cups and set aside. Pour remaining 2 cups into glass jar, cover and return to refrigerator. Mix the ½ cup warm water, 1 teaspoon sugar, ½ teaspoon ginger and 1 package dry yeast. Set in warm place until foaming nicely. Pour the 2 cups reserved starter into mixing bowl. Add 1 cup milk scalded and cooled to just warm, 4 tablespoons brown sugar or sorghum and 2 cups buckwheat flour. Beat thoroughly. Add the dry yeast mixture and beat again. Add 4 tablespoons soft butter, 1½ teaspoons salt and 3 cups white flour. Stir until the dough clears the bowl.

Spread remaining 1 cup white flour on pastry board. Turn out dough and knead well using only enough flour to make a smooth, nonsticky dough. Return to bowl, brush top of dough with butter, cover and set in warm place to rise. Turn out, knead lightly, divide and shape as desired. Place in generously buttered pans, brush tops with butter, cover and let stand in warm place until light. Bake in oven preheated to 375 degrees for about 45 minutes for small loaves. Five minutes before the end of the baking period brush tops of loaves with cream or canned milk which will make the crust a rich, russet color. This recipe will make 4 high, well-rounded small loaves.

It is nice to bake part of this dough in the large No. 2½ tin cans to make attractive sandwich slices and, also, for making French toast which is as good as any buckwheat griddlecakes ever served. Then try tiny tea buns, 20 to a 5½ x 8½ pan, each with its own little quarter-size dollop of nut topping. For this grate or grind 1 cup nuts (filberts preferred). Moisten with enough sweetened condensed milk to which a few drops of vanilla or almond flavoring has been added, to make a thick paste. Form into little patties. Place on top of buns as soon as taken from oven and brown under broiler until lightly toasted. Watch carefully to avoid overbrowning. There is nothing better to serve with tea and fresh mixed fruit.

Four-Way Sweet Bread Dough

2 cups starter
1½ cups cold water
1½ cups white flour

½ cup warm water
1 teaspoon sugar
½ teaspoon ginger
1 package dry yeast
1 cup dried skim milk
   powder

4 to 6 egg yolks plus warm
   water to make 2 cups
½ cup sugar
3 cups white flour
½ cup soft lard
1½ teaspoons salt
5 cups white flour

Empty starter from glass jar into large mixing bowl (do not use metal or plastic). Add 1½ cups cold water and 1½ cups white flour. Beat thoroughly. Cover tightly (clinging transparent wrap is good) and set in warm place (about 80°F.) overnight. Wash and scald starter jar and lid. Allow to air out overnight.

In the morning stir the starter thoroughly. Pour off 2 cups and set aside. Pour remaining 2 cups into glass jar, cover and return to refrigerator. Mix the ½ cup warm water, 1 teaspoon sugar, ½ teaspoon ginger and 1 package dry yeast. Set in warm place until foaming nicely. Pour the 2 cups reserved starter into mixing bowl. Add 1 cup dried skim milk. Beat the egg yolks (the more yolks the more tender and flaky the texture) in a measuring cup and add enough warm water to make 2 cups. Add to the starter mixture with ½ cup sugar and 3 cups white flour. Beat well. Add the dry yeast mixture as soon as it is ready and beat thoroughly. Add ½ cup soft lard, 1½ teaspoons salt and 3 cups white flour. Stir until the dough clears the bowl.

Spread the remaining 2 cups white flour on the pastry board. Turn out dough and knead thoroughly using a little more flour if necessary to make a smooth nonsticky but not too stiff dough. Return to bowl. Grease top of dough, cover and set in warm place to rise. When light turn out dough and knead well. Divide into four even portions to make up in the following ways: Old World Lemon Cookies, Grenadine Slices, Cardamom Rolls and Raisin Log. (If fillings have been prepared ahead of time and the other ingredients needed set out while the dough is rising, it will take only about 20 minutes to get all of these made up and into the pans. If they are made in order listed they will be ready for oven at spaced intervals.)

Old World Lemon Cookies

1 portion Four-Way Sweet Bread dough	½ to 1 cup Lemon Cheese (recipe below)
Grated rind of 1 lemon	1 egg white
1 teaspoon lemon extract	Sugar

Prepare Lemon Cheese ahead of time. Flatten ball of dough, sprinkle grated rind and lemon extract over it and knead it until well distributed. Roll dough out very thin (about ⅛ inch) and cut into 3-inch, or larger, rounds. Place on lightly greased flat pans so that they will not touch. Let stand about 10 minutes. Press centers to make slight depression to hold ½ teaspoon Lemon Cheese (more for larger rounds). Spread beaten egg white around rim and sprinkle lightly with sugar. Bake in oven preheated to 350°F. for at least 30 minutes until delicately tinted and the glaze has crystallized. The longer they are left in the oven to become drier and crisper the more delicious they are. There is nothing better to serve, still slightly warm from the oven, with hot spiced tea.

Lemon Cheese

Mix together in saucepan 2 cups white sugar, grated rind and juice of 3 large lemons, 3 large whole eggs (beaten), ¼ teaspoon salt and ¼ cup butter. Cook over slow heat, stirring constantly until thick. Yield: about 2½-3 cups. This can be sealed in jars to keep like jelly or will keep indefinitely in covered container in refrigerator. It is nice to have on hand at all times for it has many uses such as topping for baked puddings, filling for tarts and jelly rolls, spread for slices of warm Sally Lunn, etc.

Grenadine Slices

1 portion Four-Way Sweet   ½ cup grenadine syrup
  Bread dough   1 cup Grape-Nuts cereal

As soon as the bread dough has started to rise mix the syrup and Grape-Nuts together so that the cereal will have time to soak up all the syrup. Roll the dough out quite thin to about 20 to 10 inches. Cut in two crosswise. Spread filling thinly over the surface leaving a 2-inch strip along one side of each square. Fold over this bare strip onto filling and continue folding until a flat roll is formed. Lay both rolls lengthwise on 10x15-inch cookie sheet with seam on underside. Flatten them by rolling with the pin until they are about 3½ inches wide and as long as the pan. Do this gently so that the filling does not break through. Brush tops with soft butter. Let stand in warm place until light. Bake in oven preheated to 325°F. about 45 minutes until the crust has a beautiful bisque tint. Glaze while still warm with a powdered sugar and White Wine Frosting. If available, decorate with a row of candy raspberries down the center of each roll so that there will be one on each 1½-inch to 2-inch slice. (If rolls are to be frozen for later use wait until they have been thawed and warmed to glaze and decorate.)

White Wine Frosting

2 tablespoons soft butter
2 tablespoons white wine
1½ cup powdered sugar
3 drops Waldmeister Essence*

and a drop or two of green coloring, or ¼ teaspoon Rose Extract and a drop or two of red coloring

Beat butter, wine and sugar together until smooth. Add preferred flavoring and carefully add the coloring for a very delicate tint.

Cardamom Rolls

1 portion Four-Way Sweet
   Bread dough
8 pods whole cardamom**

1 egg yolk
1 teaspoon cream or canned milk

Remove cardamom seeds from pods and crush in mortar or place in small plastic bag and use rolling pin. Flatten the ball of dough. Sprinkle crushed seeds over surface and knead until evenly distributed through the dough. Divide in twelve pieces and shape as desired for muffin tins. They can be made into a plain ball and then, after the top is generously buttered, cut deeply with a Kaiser cutter or slashed with a deep cross in the top with sharp knife or scissors. They are also nice made up in brioche shape. Cut off about ¼ of the dough and make a tiny ball to place firmly on top of the larger ball before brushing all over with butter. When light, bake for about 25 minutes in oven preheated to 350°F. About 5 minutes before the end of the baking period brush the tops of the rolls with the egg yolk and cream beaten together. Bake to a beautiful, golden, glossy brown. These rolls are perfect for serving with a chilled fresh fruit salad and whipped cheese spread.

---

* See Sources of Supply.
** 1 teaspoon of ground cardamom can be used but it takes away the attractive appearance the flecks of crushed seed give to the rolls.

Raisin Log

1 portion Four-Way Sweet
  Bread dough
2 tablespoons canned milk
1 cup golden or dark raisins
3 tablespoons vanilla sugar*
1 teaspoon cinnamon
½ teaspoon allspice

Topping:
3 teaspoons sugar
1 teaspoon cinnamon
¼ teaspoon allspice
1 teaspoon cornstarch

Roll the dough into a rectangle with the width equal to the length of the pan (medium-size loaf) and about twice as long. Brush with canned milk. Scatter raisins over surface. Mix vanilla sugar, cinnamon and allspice together and sprinkle on evenly. (If vanilla sugar is not available, dribble 1 teaspoon of vanilla extract over dough.) Roll up tightly but do not seal ends. Place seam-side down in pan. Butter top generously and push sharp-pointed knife down through the dough almost to bottom at regular intervals to allow air bubbles between layers to escape. Set in warm place to rise and when ready for the oven, spread with the well-mixed topping (the cornstarch will help to bind the topping to the crust so that it will not crack off badly when sliced). Bake in oven preheated to 350°F. for 50 to 60 minutes. Cool before slicing.

---

* See p. 120.

Banana Flake Pecan Bread

2 cups starter
1½ cups cold water
1½ cups white flour

½ cup warm water
1 teaspoon sugar
½ teaspoon ginger
1 package dry yeast
1 cup warm water
1 cup dried skim milk
  powder

4 tablespoon sugar
½ to 1 cup dried banana
  flakes*
3 cups white flour
2 eggs, well-beaten
1½ teaspoons salt
4 tablespoons soft butter
1 cup pecans, finely chopped
5 cups white flour

Empty starter from glass jar into large mixing bowl (do not use metal or plastic). Add 1½ cups cold water and 1½ cups white flour. Beat thoroughly. Cover tightly (clinging transparent wrap is good) and set in warm place (about 80°F.) overnight. Wash and scald starter jar and lid. Allow to air out overnight.

In the morning stir the starter thoroughly. Pour off 2 cups and set aside. Pour remaining 2 cups into glass jar, cover and return to refrigerator. Mix the ½ cup warm water, 1 teaspoon sugar, ½ teaspoon ginger and 1 package dry yeast. Set in warm place until foaming nicely. Pour the 2 cups reserved starter into mixing bowl. Add 1 cup warm water, 1 cup dried milk, 4 table-spoons sugar, the banana flakes (these are very sweet and highly flavored so it would be wise to use the smaller amount the first time, then increase in later bakings if desired) and 3 cups white flour. Beat thoroughly. Add the yeast mixture as soon as ready and beat well. Add the 2 well-beaten eggs, 1½ teaspoons salt, 4 tablespoons butter, 1 cup chopped pecans and 4 cups white flour. Stir until the mixture clears the bowl.

---

* See Sources of Supply.

Spread remaining 1 cup white flour on pastry board. Turn out dough. Knead thoroughly using a little more flour if necessary. Return to bowl, brush top of dough with butter, cover and set in warm place to rise. When light, turn out, knead lightly, divide and shape as desired. Place in greased or Teflon-coated pans, brush tops with butter and set in warm place to rise. Bake in oven preheated to 350 degrees about 40 minutes for small loaves, 20 to 25 for rolls. This recipe will make 4 high, well-rounded small loaves and 1 medium-size Swedish style coffee ring or a pan of tiny tea buns to be glazed.

Polish Babka

2 cups starter
1½ cups cold water
1½ cups white flour

½ cup warm water
1 teaspoon sugar
½ teaspoon ginger
1 package dry yeast
1 cup sugar

13 egg yolks, well beaten
3 cups white flour
4 tablespoons soft butter
1½ teaspoons salt
2 teaspoons almond extract
4 cups white flour
½ cup fine rusk crumbs or
     coconut meal*

Empty starter from glass jar into large mixing bowl (do not use metal or plastic). Add 1½ cups cold water and 1½ cups white flour. Beat thoroughly. Cover bowl tightly (clinging transparent wrap is good) and set in warm place (about 80°F.) overnight. Wash and scald starter jar and lid. Allow to air out overnight.

In the morning stir the starter thoroughly. Pour off 2 cups and set aside. Pour remaining 2 cups into glass jar, cover and return

---

* See Sources of Supply.

to refrigerator. Mix ½ cup warm water, 1 teaspoon sugar, ½
teaspoon ginger and 1 package dry yeast. Set in warm place
until foaming nicely. Pour the 2 cups reserved starter into mixing bowl. Add 1 cup sugar, 13 well-beaten egg yolks and 3 cups
white flour. Beat well. Add the dry yeast mixture as soon as
ready and beat again. Add 4 tablespoons soft butter, 1½ teaspoons salt, 2 teaspoons almond extract and 3 cups white flour.
Mix well until dough clears the bowl. Spread the remaining 1
cup white flour on pastry board. Turn out dough. Knead well,
using a little more flour if necessary to make a satin-smooth
but not too stiff dough. Return to bowl, butter top of dough,
cover and let rise in warm place until dent remains when dough
is pushed with finger. Turn out and knead well again. The dough
will be very bubbly and squeaky as it is worked. Divide and
shape as desired.

This recipe will make 3 Babkas in 8-inch ring pans. The
heavier the pans the more beautiful the crust will be. Butter
pans generously and dust with crumbs or meal. Shape dough
into even roll as long as circumference of pan. Lay around the
center and push ends together. Butter top of dough and dust
with crumbs or meal. Set in warm place, cover and let rise until
dent remains in dough when pushed. Bake in oven preheated
to 325 degrees for 1 hour if using heavy pans and 45 minutes
for light-weight pans.

I prefer to make 1 large Babka, using a 3-cup portion of
dough, in a heavy cast-aluminum 9-inch Bundt pan*. There are
many delightful ways to serve this bread. One of the nicest is
to place a thick, freshly-warmed slice spread generously with
whipped butter on the plate with a beautiful frozen salad such
as Spiced Peach and Cream Cheese. The rest of the dough may
be used for any of the following recipes.

---

* See Sources of Supply.

Oven Toasties

When Babka dough has rested for about 20 minutes after kneading so that it will roll out easily, pat out a 1-cup portion on a sheet of waxed paper which has been dusted with flour. Then roll evenly to fit a 10 x 15-inch cookie sheet. Have pan very lightly buttered if not using Teflon-coated one. Roll dough over into pan, gently peel off paper and press into corners and along edges to completely cover surface. Spread with 1 cup very thick apple butter (preferably the rosy-red homemade kind). Roll out a second 1-cup portion of dough in the same manner on waxed paper and place on top of filling as evenly as possible. Brush top lightly with butter and then cut with sharp knife or pastry cutter into 18 sections or 12 larger ones. Cut a cross in center of each section. Let stand in warm place until slightly risen. Cut through between sections again to be sure all are separated. Bake in oven preheated to 325°F. for about 45 minutes until a beautiful golden brown and dry. Remove from pan and cool before storing. They freeze perfectly and should be placed in oven or under broiler to toast lightly before serving.

Dessert Rolls

Use a 1½-cup portion of Babka dough to make 12 muffin-shaped rolls in small tins. Allow to rise very light. Bake in oven preheated to 325°F. for about 25 minutes. These can be treated as individual Babas au Rhum: pour hot fruit and rum syrup over them. Allow to stand until all liquid has been soaked up. This will take several hours and it is even better to let them stand overnight. Serve with whipped cream or other topping. For another way to serve, remove centers with sharp knife. Fill with marshmallow creme, replace top crusts, place in dessert dishes and spoon over them any bright tart fruit sauce.

Sweet Topper Rolls

1½ cups Babka dough
4 cinnamon coated graham
  crackers
2 tablespoons sugar
1 teaspoon cinnamon

½ teaspoon instant coffee
½ cup finely chopped nuts
3 teaspoons cream or
  canned milk

Divide dough into 12 equal portions. Shape into balls, roll in melted butter then in the mixture of graham cracker crumbs, sugar, cinnamon and instant coffee. Place in well greased muffin tins. Make a depression well down in center of each roll and fill with the chopped nuts topped with remaining crumb mixture. Let rise until very light. Press filling down lightly and drip ¼ teaspoon cream or canned milk over it. Bake in oven preheated to 325°F. for about 25 minutes. The filling will rise above the top of the roll and when nicely browned is as crunchy and rich as butter brickle candy.

Triple Treat Braid

2 cups Babka dough
2 tablespoons honey
2 tablespoons soft butter
½ teaspoon ginger
3 tablespoons fine dry
  bread crumbs
12 large soft dates

⅓ cup finely chopped
  English walnuts
1 teaspoon powdered
  orange concentrate*
⅓ cup strawberry preserves
⅓ cup Grape-Nuts cereal

Roll dough into rectangle the length of the cookie sheet and about 9 inches wide. Cut into 3 strips lengthwise. Mix the honey, butter, ginger and bread crumbs together and spread on center

---

* See p. 91.

of first strip. Cut dates in half lengthwise and lay on center of second strip. Sprinkle over them the finely chopped nuts and orange concentrate. Mix strawberry preserves and cereal together. Spread on center of third strip. Moisten edges of each strip and seal tightly. Lay side by side on sheet. Start in middle and braid to each end. Brush top with butter. Let stand until very light. Bake in oven preheated to 325°F. about 45 minutes until very well done. Brush top of braid with cream or canned milk about 5 minutes before the end of the baking period. This bread is every bit as delicious and attractive as the many-flavored strudel which used to be among our Christmas goodies every year and which takes so many hours to make.

Twin Bread Sponge

2 cups starter	½ teaspoon ginger
1½ cups cold water	1 package dry yeast
1½ cups white flour	2 cups buttermilk, scalded and cooled
½ cup warm water	3 cups white flour
1 teaspoon sugar	

Empty starter from glass jar into large mixing bowl (do not use metal or plastic). Add 1½ cups cold water and 1½ cups white flour. Beat thoroughly. Cover bowl tightly (clinging transparent wrap is good) and set in warm place (about 80°F.) overnight. Wash and scald starter jar and lid. Allow to air out overnight.

In the morning stir the starter thoroughly. Pour off 2 cups and set aside. Pour remaining 2 cups into glass jar, cover and return to refrigerator. Mix ½ cup warm water, 1 teaspoon sugar, ½ teaspoon ginger and 1 package dry yeast. Set in warm place until foaming nicely. Pour the 2 cups reserved starter into mixing bowl. Add 2 cups buttermilk, scalded and cooled to just

warm and 3 cups white flour. Beat well. Add the dry yeast mixture as soon as it is ready and beat thoroughly. Now divide the
sponge and place half (3 cups) in another mixing bowl. With
one half make Hickory Smoked Corn Bread and with the other
Rolled Wheat Peanut Bread.

Hickory Smoked Corn Bread

½ Twin Bread sponge	4 tablespoons bacon fat
2½ cups white flour	2 cups hickory smoked
2 eggs, well-beaten	stone-ground corn meal*
4 tablespoons sugar	1½ teaspoons salt

Spread 1 cup of the white flour on pastry board. Mix all other
ingredients together, stirring until the dough clears the bowl.
Turn out on board and knead well using a little more white flour if
necessary (amount depends on coarseness of corn meal). Return
to bowl, grease top of dough, cover and let rise in warm place
for 30 minutes. Turn out, knead lightly, divide and shape as desired. Place in greased pans, brush tops with bacon fat or butter, cover and set in warm place to rise. When very light bake
in oven preheated to 400°F. After 20 minutes reduce heat to
350 degrees and continue baking about 25 minutes for small
loaves and 5 to 10 minutes longer for rolls, depending on their
size. This recipe will make 3 small loaves slightly rounded above
the pan rim. Sixteen good-sized crescent rolls can be made
from ⅓ of the dough.

---

* If the prepared hickory smoked corn meal is not available, hickory
smoked seasoning salt may be used instead of the plain salt called for with
regular fine yellow corn meal.

Rolled Wheat Peanut Bread

½ Twin Bread sponge
1½ cups white flour
5 tablespoons Burnt Sugar
   Syrup (recipe below)

1½ teaspoons salt
½ cup chunky-style peanut
   butter
2 cups rolled whole wheat

Spread ¾ cup of the white flour on pastry board. Mix all other ingredients together, including remaining flour, stirring until the dough clears the bowl. Turn out on board. Knead well using a little more flour if necessary. Return to bowl, grease top of dough, cover and let rise in warm place for 30 minutes. Turn out, knead lightly, divide and shape as desired. Place in greased pans, brush tops with butter and set in warm place to rise. When very light bake in oven preheated to 400°F. After 20 minutes reduce heat to 350° and continue baking about 25 minutes longer for small loaves, 5 to 10 minutes for miniature loaves. This recipe will make 2 high, well-rounded small loaves and 3 miniature loaves which children enjoy greatly with jelly and hot chocolate.

Burnt Sugar Syrup

Melt ¼ cup white sugar in heavy saucepan, stirring constantly until it is clear deep amber color. Stir in ⅓ cup hot water a few drops at a time, being very careful for it makes a great deal of steam. Continue simmering until all lumps are melted. Remove from heat and cool to just warm before using. This is the amount to use in this bread but the syrup is so nice to use in many ways that you could use 1 cup sugar and 1⅓ cups water. It can be stored in a glass jar in the refrigerator indefinitely.

Lemon Angel Bread

2 cups starter
1½ cups cold water
1½ cups white flour

½ cup warm water
1 teaspoon sugar
½ teaspoon ginger
1 package dry yeast
3 teaspoons lemon extract

1 cup warm water
1 cup dried skim milk
  powder
3 cups white flour
½ cup soft lard
1½ teaspoons salt
6 egg whites
1 cup powdered sugar
5 cups white flour

Empty starter from glass jar into large mixing bowl (do not use metal or plastic). Add 1½ cups cold water and 1½ cups white flour. Beat thoroughly. Cover tightly (clinging transparent wrap is good) and set in warm place (about 80°F.) overnight. Wash and scald starter jar and lid. Allow to air out overnight.

In the morning stir the starter thoroughly. Pour off 2 cups and set aside. Pour remaining 2 cups into glass jar, cover and return to refrigerator. Mix the ½ cup warm water, 1 teaspoon sugar, ½ teaspoon ginger and 1 package dry yeast. Set in warm place until foaming nicely. Pour the 2 cups reserved starter into mixing bowl. All 3 teaspoons lemon extract, 1 cup warm water, 1 cup dried skim milk and 3 cups white flour. Beat well. Add the dry yeast mixture as soon as ready. Mix well. Add ½ cup soft lard (shortening may be omitted if desired—the taste will be just as delicious but crust will not be as tender) and 1½ teaspoons salt. Mix well.

Beat 6 egg whites with rotary beater until they will hold a peak. Beat in the 1 cup powdered sugar a little at a time and continue until whites are as stiff as for angel food cake. Fold into batter. Add 3 cups white flour and stir until the dough clears the bowl. Spread remaining 2 cups white flour on the pastry board. Turn out dough which will be quite soft. Turn up around edges with plate scraper until well floured. Knead gently but thoroughly using as much flour as necessary to make a smooth nonsticky dough. Return to bowl. Grease top of dough, cover and set in warm place until light. Turn out, knead lightly, divide and shape as desired. Place in greased or Teflon-coated pans. Either brush tops of loaves with butter or roll top in flour before placing in pan. Cover with light cloth and allow to rise in warm place. This will rise more in the oven than plain dough so it should be put in before it quite reaches the rim of the pans. Bake in oven preheated to 350 degrees for about 45 minutes for medium loaves. This recipe will make 4 high, well-rounded medium loaves.

Rose Petal Bread

For 2 small loaves flatten a 3-cup portion of Lemon Angel dough. Sprinkle over it 1 teaspoon rose extract and 1 cup (lightly packed) dried, crushed rose petals. Work evenly through the dough. Divide and shape into loaves. Place in greased pans, brush tops with butter, cover and let rise in warm place. When light, bake as directed above.

This bread has a most delightful fragrance with just a hint of flavor to the taste and the slices are very attractive, flecked with the varicolored bits of petals. Dainty sandwiches made with plain whipped cream cheese are perfect with hot tea.

Rosebud Rolls

Roll a 1½- to 2-cup portion of Lemon Angel dough to about ⅛ thickness. Cut into 2-inch circles for small muffin tins and 2½ inch for larger tins. Lap 5 circles around the inside of each form and fold 1 circle in fourths to stand in center. Brush edges generously with melted butter. When very light and puffy bake in oven preheated to 350°F. (325° for Teflon-coated pans) for about 25 minutes. If desired spread edges of petals with pastel tinted glaze while still slightly warm.

Dutch Krispies

Use 1 cup Lemon Angel dough* for each 10 x 15-inch pan. Roll out very thin to about 12 x 15 inches. Brush ⅔ surface very lightly with butter. Fold uncoated ⅓ over center of rectangle and the other end over this. Now fold ⅓ of this rectangle under and ⅓ over making 9 layers of dough. Roll out on lightly floured waxed paper to about 10 x 15 inches. Lift by one side of paper and flip over onto lightly greased bottom of flat pan turned upside down or flat cookie sheet. Pat with fingers to even up edges and square the corners. Brush surface generously with 1 egg white beaten with 1 teaspoon almond extract. Sprinkle heavily with fine or medium sugar crystals. Cut into squares with pastry wheel or sharp knife. Let stand for about 20 minutes. Bake in oven preheated to 325°F. for about 35 minutes until well baked and the glaze is golden. Remove from oven, separate squares, turn upside down and replace on pan. Turn off heat and when oven has cooled slightly, return pan to oven and leave until squares are completely dry and crisp. These can be kept indefinitely in freezer or canister or even a plastic bag. They are just wonderful with coffee any time.

---

* See recipe page 88.

Fig Swirls

1½ cups Lemon Angel
   dough
6 large dried figs
¼ cup brown sugar
¼ cup concentrated cereal
   flakes*

1 teaspoon powdered
   orange drink
   concentrate**

Prepare filling by soaking figs overnight in just enough hot water to cover. In the morning pour off liquid and save for other cooking uses. Chop figs finely, add the ¼ cup brown sugar, ¼ cup cereal flakes and 1 teaspoon orange concentrate. Mix well and let stand to thicken while dough is being made. For 8 large swirls roll the dough out into a square 12 x 12 inches. Spread generously with soft butter. Cut into 8 even strips with pastry wheel or knife. Twist each strip as it is laid in a circle on lightly buttered cookie sheet. Flatten center end of each swirl to make a depression for the filling. Divide fig filling evenly among the 8 swirls. Sprinkle twisted rims with sugar and cinnamon or leave plain and glaze with powdered-sugar icing after baking. Let stand until very light. Bake in oven preheated to 325°F. about 25 minutes. It saves time to make up 4 times this amount of filling as it will keep indefinitely in refrigerator container and can be used in many ways such as spreading a layer over a bread pudding which is to be topped with meringue.

---

* "Concentrate," a Kellogg Cereal Company product.
** Orange-flavored instant breakfast drink, such as "Tang," a General Foods product.

Milk Pastry Bread

2 cups starter
1½ cups cold water
1½ cups white flour

½ cup warm water
1 teaspoon sugar
½ teaspoon ginger
1 package dry yeast
2 cups scalded and cooled milk

½ cup sugar
3 cups white flour
4 tablespoons rice polish
4 tablespoons soft butter
1½ teaspoons salt
2 eggs, well-beaten
4½ cups white flour

Empty starter from glass jar into large mixing bowl (do not use metal or plastic). Add 1½ cups cold water and 1½ cups white flour. Beat thoroughly. Cover tightly (clinging transparent wrap is good) and set in warm place (about 80°F.) overnight. Wash and scald starter jar and lid. Allow to air out overnight.

In the morning stir the starter thoroughly. Pour off 2 cups and set aside. Pour remaining 2 cups into glass jar, cover and return to refrigerator. Mix the ½ cup warm water, 1 teaspoon sugar, ½ teaspoon ginger and 1 package dry yeast. Set in warm place until foaming nicely. Pour the 2 cups reserved starter into mixing bowl. Add the 2 cups scalded and cooled milk, ½ cup sugar, 3 cups white flour and 4 tablespoons rice polish. Beat well. Add the dry yeast mixture as soon as ready. Beat thoroughly. Add 4 tablespoons soft butter, 1½ teaspoons salt and 2 well-beaten eggs. Mix well. Add 3½ cups white flour and stir until dough clears the bowl.

Spread the remaining 1 cup flour on the pastry board. Turn out dough and knead well using a little more flour if necessary to make a smooth, nonsticky dough. Return to bowl. Butter top of dough, cover and set in warm place to rise. When light turn out dough, knead lightly, divide and shape as desired. Place in buttered pans, brush tops with butter and set in warm place until light. Bake in oven preheated to 350 degrees for 45 to 50 minutes for medium loaves. This recipe makes 4 high, well-rounded medium loaves.

This dough can be used to make many kinds of pastries as tender and flaky as can be, easily and quickly.

Note: Rice polish is a fine powder containing the germ. It can be used in any bread just as wheat germ is added for more food value. It seems to me it gives a soft bread more body and tenderness. Slightly less flour is needed when it is added to a recipe which does not call for it but this can be easily taken care of when kneading the last amount of flour into the dough.

Cheese Puffs

2 cups Milk Pastry dough   Various condiments for
6 ounces cheese spread   toppings

Roll dough out to about ⅛-inch thickness in a rectangle about 3 times as long as wide. Spread ⅔ of the surface with the cheese spread (Gorgonzola with brandy is a favorite). Fold the unspread ⅓ of rectangle over center ⅓ and lap remaining section over this. Now fold ⅓ of this 3-thickness rectangle underneath and the remaining section over top. This gives 9 thicknesses of dough. Slip into plastic bag and lay in refrigerator until slightly chilled. Then roll out into a 16 x 6-inch rectangle and cut evenly into 2-inch squares for 24 puffs. Use Teflon-coated cookie sheets if possible. If not, place on very lightly

oiled pans. Brush tops lightly with butter and sprinkle with whatever condiment is desired. It is nice to use four different ones
such as seasoned pepper, garlic salt, celery salt, and barbecue
seasoning, topping 6 puffs with each. Let stand until very
puffy and light. Bake in oven preheated to 350°F. for about
25 minutes letting them brown no darker than a soda cracker.
While still warm they may be slit on one side and stuffed with
any preferred soft filling such as deviled ham or chicken or
other homemade ground meat filling.

These puffs, freshly warmed, are wonderful for an outdoor supper with hot tomato bouillon, chilled salmon salad and a big
bowl of mixed lettuce and cress to be eaten plain or dipped in
sour cream and chive dressing. If anyone has room for dessert,
old-fashioned Maids of Honor make a perfect ending for this
meal.

Maids of Honor

1 cup Milk Pastry dough	1 cup sugar
Soft lard	4 tablespoons soft butter
Raspberry or other jam	1 cup ground nuts
4 eggs	1 tablespoon lemon juice
¼ cup flour	¼ teaspoon mace

Roll 1 cup Milk Pastry dough very thin. Spread ⅔ surface
lightly with soft lard. Fold unspread ⅓ over center. Fold other
side over on top. Now fold ⅓ of this 3-thickness rectangle underneath and the remaining section over top. This gives 9 thicknesses of dough. Slip into plastic bag and lay in refrigerator
until slightly chilled. Roll out as thin as for pie crust. Cut into
circles and place over the bottoms of individual custard cups or
muffin tins turned upside down and press lightly to shape but do

not stretch. Even small tin cans such as deviled ham comes in can be used as they are much easier to work around than muffin tins. The circles should be at least 2 inches wider than the diameter of the form they are to be used over. After all are prepared cover with a thin cloth or sheet of transparent wrap and let stand for 20 minutes while preparing filling.

Before placing in oven prick the dough with sharp fork tines over what will be the bottoms of the tarts. Bake in oven preheated to 350°F. just until done enough to hold shape and beginning to brown. Remove from oven, turn right side up on cookie sheet. Place 1 tablespoon jam in the bottom of each shell and divide the filling among them. Turn oven up to 400 degrees, bake for 10 minutes and then turn oven back to 350 degrees and bake for 10 minutes more or until the filling has become firm to the touch. Serve slightly warm or cold with whipped cream or ice cream.

To prepare the filling: Beat the 4 eggs until very light. Sift the ¼ cup flour with 1 cup sugar and beat into eggs. Add 1 cup of ground nuts mixed with 4 tablespoons soft butter, 1 tablespoon lemon juice and ¼ teaspoon mace. Stir well and spoon into shells on top of jam.

Cherry Cheese Tarts

Prepare shells as directed for Maids of Honor. Bake until completely done and brown as desired. Remove from forms and cool. Coat insides of shells with layers of whipped cream cheese. Fill with commercial canned cherry pie filling. Top with small rosette of cheese or whipped topping and chill before serving.

Large pie shells can be made in the same way by turning the pan upside down, then turning shell right side up into next larger-size pan.

Millet Diet Bread

2 cups starter
1½ cups cold water
1½ cups white flour

½ cup warm water
⅛ teaspoon liquid artificial
    sweetener
½ teaspoon ginger
1 package dry yeast
1 cup warm water

1 teaspoon liquid artificial
    sweetener
1 cup dried skim milk
    powder
½ cup gluten flour*
2 cups millet flour*
4 tablespoons safflower oil
1½ teaspoons salt (may be
    omitted)
3 cups natural white flour*

Empty starter from glass jar into large mixing bowl (do not use metal or plastic). Add 1½ cups cold water and 1½ cups white flour. Mix thoroughly, cover tightly (clinging transparent wrap is good) and set in warm place (about 80°F.) overnight. Wash and scald starter jar and lid. Allow to air out overnight.

In the morning stir the starter thoroughly. Pour off 2 cups and set aside. Pour remainder of starter into jar; cover and return to refrigerator. Mix the ½ cup warm water, ⅛ teaspoon liquid sweetener (equal to 1 teaspoon sugar), ½ teaspoon ginger and 1 package dry yeast. Set in warm place until foaming nicely. Pour the 2 cups reserved starter into mixing bowl. Add 1 cup warm water, 1 teaspoon liquid sweetener (equal to 8 teaspoons sugar) 1 cup dried skim milk, ½ cup gluten flour and 2 cups millet flour. Beat thoroughly. Add the yeast mixture as soon as ready and beat well. Add 4 tablespoons safflower oil, 1½ teaspoons salt (if permitted in diet) and 2 cups natural white flour. Stir until the dough clears the bowl. Spread remaining 1 cup natural white flour on the pastry board. Turn out dough and

* See Sources of Supply.

knead well for several minutes, using only enough flour to make a smooth nonsticky dough. Return to bowl, oil top of dough, cover and set in warm place to rise. When light, turn out, knead lightly, divide and shape as desired. Place in oiled pans, brush tops with oil, cover with cloth and set in warm place to rise. When very light (this bread rises quickly so watch carefully) bake in oven preheated to 400 degrees, about 45 minutes for small loaves and 25 minutes for muffin-type rolls. This recipe makes 4 high, well-rounded small loaves.

The crust will be hard to the touch but browns beautifully and is crisp and crunchy—so good with fresh, tart gooseberry jam. The crust is even more delicious for those who can have salt if the sides and bottoms of some of the oiled pans are sprinkled lightly with fine salt. Also sprinkle the tops of the loaves.

Crusty Bread Sticks

For the crustiest of bread sticks so good with a bland soup like Cream of Tomato accompanied by generous slices of smoked cheese, shape small portions of dough into a little larger than pencil-sized rolls about 6 inches long. Roll firmly in coarsely crushed sea-salt crytals. Place on cookie sheets (best when baked on Teflon-coated sheet). Slip into large plastic bag to keep from drying. Let rise until dent remains when dough is pushed. Carefully roll over. Bake in oven preheated to 400 degrees until biscuit-tan, with pan of boiling water on floor of oven. As soon as colored, turn off heat, remove pan of water and allow sticks to remain in oven until completely dry and crisp.

Picnic Cakes

2 cups starter	1 teaspoon sugar
1½ cups cold water	½ teaspoon ginger
1½ cups white flour	1 package dry yeast
	1½ cups white flour
½ cup warm water	1 cup warm water

Empty starter from glass jar into large mixing bowl (do not use metal or plastic). Add 1½ cups cold water and 1½ cups flour. Beat thoroughly, cover tightly (clinging transparent wrap is good) and set in warm place overnight (about 80°F). Wash and scald starter jar and lid. Allow to air out overnight.

In the morning beat starter thoroughly. Pour off 2 cups and set aside. Pour remaining 2 cups starter into glass jar, cover and return to refrigerator. Mix ½ cup warm water, 1 teaspoon sugar, ½ teaspoon ginger and 1 package dry yeast. Set in warm place until foaming nicely. Add 1½ cups white flour and 1 cup warm water to starter and beat well. Add the yeast mixture as soon as ready and beat again. Now divide this batter in halves and use two mixing bowls. If you do not wish to make both cakes the same morning, half of the batter can be made into plain white bread by using ½ the remaining ingredients that one would use for a full recipe. However, if all the ingredients for both cakes are measured and set out ready to use (chocolate melted, nuts chopped, etc.) both cakes can be ready for the pans in a very short time.

Chocolate Cake

½ Picnic Cake batter
2½ cups flour
1 teaspoon cinnamon
1 teaspoon instant coffee
2 eggs, well-beaten
¾ cup dried buttermilk
  powder

1 teaspoon salt
1 cup sugar
4 tablespoons soft butter
2 squares melted chocolate

Sift the 2½ cups flour with 1 teaspoon each of cinnamon and instant coffee. Add all the ingredients to the batter and beat thoroughly. It will be quite stiff but still workable. Cover bowl and let stand 20 minutes. Stir thoroughly and spoon into buttered pans. Smooth out as well as possible with spoon, then brush top of dough with butter. Pat dough smooth and even with fingers. Cover with transparent wrap drawn tight so it will not sag and touch dough. Set in warm place and let rise until very light. Bake in oven preheated to 350°F. about 45 minutes for sheet cakes and 20 minutes for small cupcakes.

This recipe will make 2 cakes in 8 x 8 x 2-inch pans and 6 small cupcakes which children love to eat as soon as cool enough, frosting them quickly with marshmallow creme right from the jar themselves. This chocolate cake is soft and feathery-light but not crumbly at all like a quick cake so it is ideal for picnics. The two cakes can be put together with marshmallow-powdered sugar frosting, with shaved sweet chocolate sprinkled over the frosting on top. This makes such a high cake, however, that it is usually more convenient to treat the layers as sheet cakes. They freeze beautifully and can be frosted after thawing very nicely.

Glorified Ginger Cake

½ Picnic Cake batter
2 cups flour
1 cup sugar
1 teaspoon cinnamon
1 teaspoon allspice
3 teaspoons ginger
1 teaspoon salt

2 eggs, well-beaten
1 cup commercial sour
cream
2 tablespoons sorghum
2½ cups flour
4 tablespoons soft butter
1 cup finely chopped nuts

Sift the 2 cups flour, 1 cup sugar with 1 teaspoon each cinnamon and allspice, 3 teaspoons ginger and 1 teaspoon salt. Set aside 1 cup of this to be used for topping. Add the remainder of the sifted mixture with the 2 well-beaten eggs, 1 cup sour cream, 2 tablespoons sorghum and 2½ cups flour to the batter. Beat thoroughly. It will be stiff but workable. Cover bowl and let rest for 20 minutes. Stir well and spoon into buttered pans. Smooth as well as possible with spoon. Then brush tops with butter and pat out smooth and even with fingers. Work the 4 tablespoons soft butter into the 1 cup of reserved mix. Stir in the chopped nuts. Sprinkle over top of cakes. Press down lightly. Cover cake with transparent wrap drawn tightly so it will not sag and touch the dough. Let rise until very light. Bake in oven preheated to 350°F., 45 minutes for sheet cakes and 20 minutes for small cupcakes. This recipe makes 2 cakes in 8 x 8 x 2-inch pans and 12 small cupcakes. I like to use all the topping for the large cakes and frost the cupcakes with various flavors as needed.

If there seems to be danger of some of the crumb topping sliding off the cake during baking, just set the pan on a sheet of heavy aluminum foil large enough to fold up higher than the sides of the pan. Fold over snugly at the corners and fasten with adhesive tape. This saves the topping, saves cleaning the oven and gives a beautifully straight-sided cake with no over-brown ridge around the edge. This cake freezes perfectly and seems to become more spicy and flavorful after aging a bit.

Coffee Malted Milk Bread

2 cups starter
1½ cups cold water
1½ cups white flour

½ cup warm water
1 teaspoon sugar
½ teaspoon ginger
1 package dry yeast
1 cup natural-flavored
   malted milk powder

3 teaspoons instant coffee
1 cup warm water
4 tablespoons sugar
3 cups white flour
2 eggs, well-beaten
4 tablespoons soft butter
2 teaspoons salt
4½ cups white flour

Empty starter from glass jar into large mixing bowl (do not use metal or plastic). Add 1½ cups cold water and 1½ cups white flour. Beat thoroughly. Cover tightly (clinging transparent wrap is good) and set in warm place (about 80°F.) overnight. Wash and scald starter jar and lid. Allow to air out overnight.

In the morning stir the starter thoroughly. Pour off 2 cups and set aside. Pour remaining 2 cups into glass jar, cover and return to refrigerator. Mix the ½ cup warm water, 1 teaspoon sugar, ½ teaspoon ginger and 1 package dry yeast. Set in warm place until foaming nicely. Pour the 2 cups reserved starter into mixing bowl. Add 1 cup natural-flavor malted milk and 3 teaspoons instant coffee stirred into 1 cup warm water. Add 4 tablespoons sugar and 3 cups white flour. Beat thoroughly. Add the dry yeast mixture as soon as ready and beat again. Add 2 eggs, well beaten, 4 tablespoons soft butter, 2 teaspoons salt and 3½ cups white flour. Stir until the mixture clears the bowl.

Spread remaining 1 cup white flour on pastry board. Turn out dough and knead thoroughly using only enough flour to make a smooth, nonsticky dough. Return to bowl, grease top of dough, cover and set in warm place to rise. When light, turn out, knead lightly, divide and shape as desired. Place in greased pans, brush tops with butter, cover and let rise until light. Bake in oven preheated to 350 degrees about 45 minutes for loaves, 20 to 25 minutes for rolls. This recipe makes 4 very high, well-rounded loaves. In fact, these loaves will be so high that enough dough can be taken from each 2-cup portion for a medium loaf to make 1 miniature loaf for each medium loaf and still have loaves as high as those from most other breads in this class.

To date, this bread is the fastest rising and has the most perfect texture of any that I have made. Malted milk contains some soda which may account for the quickness of the dough. It also contains lecithin, a derivative of soybeans, which gives added food value. The amount of instant coffee used gives just the faintest suggestion of flavor and aroma. More may be used if desired or vanilla, almond or caramel flavoring may be used instead of the coffee.

Vanilla Rusks

For each loaf use 1 cup Coffee Malted Milk dough. Roll out into rectangle about 4 x 10 inches with very straight and even ends. Fold ⅓ width over center, then fold other side over top and seal. Slit a 3-inch length of vanilla bean, scrape out seeds and mix with 2 teaspoons white sugar. Spread in strip as long as dough on waxed paper. Gently lift dough and roll in the sugar mixture. Place on Teflon-coated or lightly-buttered cookie sheet (one sheet will hold two of these long loaves). Let rise until very light. It will spread to about 4 inches in width. Bake in oven preheated to 325°F. for about 30 minutes until lightly browned. Remove from oven and cool. Cut into about ⅓-inch thick slices. Spread on flat pans and return to warm oven. Dry, turning over several times, until completely crisp throughout. This will keep in cookie jar for some time or store in plastic bags in freezer. One half teaspoon coffee, cinnamon or other spice may be used in place of vanilla.

Fruit Log

Roll out a 2-cup portion of Coffee Malted Milk dough into a long, thin rectangle with width equal to length of loaf pan. Sprinkle ½ cup each of golden and dark raisins and 2 tablespoons finely chopped candied ginger over the surface. Press lightly into position, then roll up and place seam-side down in lightly buttered medium loaf pan. Brush top with butter. Leave plain, sprinkle with sugar and spice or glaze after baking in oven preheated to 350°F. for about 45 minutes.

The following 5 recipes contain flavored gelatins. I was searching for something to add flavor and color to special-occasion breads when I thought of trying this product. I am very pleased with the results not only because of the attractive appearance and delicious taste but, also, because of the added food value.

This, I am assured, is not affected by the baking temperatures. The nutritionist for a nationally known brand of flavor gelatin supplied an analysis of the elements of each flavor (I was surprised to learn that not all the flavors contain the same percentage of constituents although the difference is not large). Perhaps the listing of an analysis of one flavor would be interesting to those who use these recipes. A 6 oz. box of lemon gelatin contains: 3 grams moisture, 13 grams protein, 0.018 grams fat, 0.78 grams ash, 140 grams carbohydrate, 5.1 grams adipic acid, and 400 milligrams sodium which all add up to 660 calories.

Tomato Salad Bread

2 cups starter	1 package dry yeast
1½ cups cold water	1 cup dried skim milk
1½ cups white flour	powder
	3 cups white flour
1 cup thick tomato juice	1 teaspoon rotisserie
1 3-ounce box salad-flavored	seasoning
gelatin	½ teaspoon celery salt
½ cup warm water	½ cup soft butter or
1 teaspoon sugar	margarine
½ teaspoon ginger	4 cups white flour

Empty starter from glass jar into large mixing bowl (do not use metal or plastic). Add 1½ cups cold water and 1½ cups white flour. Beat thoroughly. Cover bowl tightly (clinging transparent wrap is good) and set in warm place (about 80°F.) overnight. Wash and scald starter jar and lid. Allow to air out overnight.

In the morning stir the starter thoroughly. Pour off 2 cups

and set aside. Pour remaining 2 cups into glass jar, cover and return to refrigerator. Heat the 1 cup tomato juice (if using the kind which separates, pour off liquid from top before measuring out 1 cup) and dissolve the gelatin in it. While it cools to just warm, mix ½ cup warm water, 1 teaspoon sugar, ½ teaspoon ginger and 1 package dry yeast. Set in warm place until foaming nicely. Pour the 2 cups reserved starter into mixing bowl. Add the cooled tomato juice mixture, 1 cup dried skim milk and 3 cups white flour. Beat thoroughly. Add the dry yeast mixture as soon as ready and beat well. Add 1 teaspoon rotisserie seasoning, ½ teaspoon celery salt, ½ cup soft shortening and 3 cups white flour. Stir until the dough clears the bowl. Spread remaining 1 cup white flour on pastry board. Turn out dough and knead well, using a little more flour if necessary to make a smooth, nonsticky dough. Return to bowl, grease top of dough, cover and set in warm place to rise. When light, turn out, knead lightly, divide and shape as desired. Place in greased pans, brush tops with butter and set in warm place to rise. When light, bake in oven preheated to 350 degrees about 45 minutes for small loaves and 20 to 25 minutes for rolls. This recipe makes 4 high, well-rounded small loaves and 12 small muffin rolls.

This bread rises very quickly and has a delightful spongecake-like texture. I like to make part of it into Coiled Loaves by making a loaf-size portion of dough (1½ cups) into a long strip about 4 inches wide. Fold over in half, roll into coil and place in 5-inch round pan seam-side down. Brush top generously with melted butter so that the rings will remain separated as they rise. For an extra beautiful crust brush with cream or canned milk about 5 minutes before end of baking period. This is a perfect companion for a green tossed salad and a variety of cheeses. The slices from the plain loaves are great with any sliced, roasted meat for picnic sandwiches.

Note: Rotisserie seasoning is a blend of seasonings sold under that name (French's, Schilling and Lawry's are some of the brands).

Hawaiian Holiday Bread

2 cups starter	1 package dry yeast
1½ cups cold water	1 cup dried skim milk
1½ cups white flour	powder
	4 tablespoons sugar
1 cup pineapple juice	3 cups white flour
1 6-ounce box orange-	2 eggs, well-beaten
pineapple gelatin	½ cup soft lard
½ cup warm water	1½ teaspoons salt
1 teaspoon sugar	4 cups white flour
½ teaspoon ginger	

Empty starter from glass jar into large mixing bowl (do not use metal or plastic). Add 1½ cups cold water and 1½ cups white flour. Beat thoroughly. Cover bowl tightly (clinging transparent wrap is good) and set in warm place (about 80°F.) overnight. Wash and scald starter jar and lid. Allow to air out overnight.

In the morning stir starter thoroughly. Pour off 2 cups and set aside. Pour remaining 2 cups into glass jar, cover and return to refrigerator. Pour off clear liquid from top of pineapple juice can and measure 1 cup from thick portion in bottom. Heat juice, dissolve gelatin in it and cool to just warm. Mix ½ cup warm water, 1 teaspoon sugar, ½ teaspoon ginger and 1 package dry yeast. Set in warm place until foaming nicely. Pour the 2 cups reserved starter into mixing bowl. Add the warm juice and gelatin, 1 cup dried milk, 4 tablespoons sugar and 3 cups white flour. Beat thoroughly. Add the yeast mixture as soon as it is ready and beat well. Add 2 well beaten eggs, ½ cup soft lard (it has no distinctive flavor to detract from the fruit flavor but butter or margarine can be used if desired), 1½ teaspoons salt and 3 cups white flour. Stir until the dough clears the bowl. Spread the remaining 1 cup white flour on pastry board. Turn out dough and knead thoroughly without using any more than necessary to make a smooth, nonsticky dough. Return to bowl, grease top, cover and set in warm place until light. Turn out, knead lightly, divide and shape as desired. Place in greased pans, brush tops with butter, cover and let rise until light. Bake in oven preheated to 350 degrees for about 45 minutes for medium loaves. This recipe makes 4 high, well-rounded medium loaves. S-shaped loaves are especially attractive.

Golden Coffee Cake

1½ cups Hawaiian Holiday dough	1 tablespoon sugar
Melted butter	¼ teaspoon mace
½ cup golden raisins	2 candied pineapple rings cut into 24 square slices
1 candied pineapple ring, finely chopped	1 tablespoon sugar
	¼ teaspoon mace

Divide dough in halves and roll out 2 thin circles to fit in 9-inch round cake pan. Place first circle in buttered pan. Brush butter over surface and sprinkle with raisins, chopped pineapple, 1 tablespoon sugar and ¼ teaspoon mace (this can be more evenly distributed if it is first stirred into the sugar). Top with the second circle of dough. Press the squares of candied pineapple deeply into the dough in three rows of 8 each in spoke pattern so that they will center each of 8 wedges when cut. Spread butter generously over candied pineapple and dough. Sprinkle with the remaining sugar and mace. Let rise until very light. Bake slowly at 325°F. for 35 to 40 minutes until well done and the top is beautifully glazed and the squares of pineapple look like glistening jewels.

Tea Tarts

1½ cups Hawaiian Holiday dough
Melted butter
12 teaspoons apricot jam

12 teaspoons shredded coconut
12 nut halves or candied cherries

Divide dough, shape into balls, dip in melted butter and place in muffin tins. Cover and let stand in warm place until about half risen. Press fingers deeply into centers, pushing dough well up around sides. Fill depression with 1 teaspoon apricot or other thick jam. Sprinkle top of each with coconut and place a half nut or candied cherry in center. Let rise until very light. Bake in oven preheated to 325°F. for about 25 minutes.

Apricot Lemon Bread

2 cups starter
1½ cups cold water
1½ cups white flour

½ cup warm water
1 teaspoon sugar
½ teaspoon ginger
1 package dry yeast
1½ cups apricot nectar

1 6-ounce box lemon-flavored gelatin
1 cup dried skim milk powder
3 cups white flour
½ cup soft butter
1½ teaspoon salt
3½ cups white flour

Empty starter from glass jar into large mixing bowl (do not use metal or plastic). Add 1½ cups cold water and 1½ cups white flour. Beat thoroughly. Cover tightly (clinging transparent wrap is good) and set in warm place (about 80°F.) overnight. Wash and scald starter jar and lid. Allow to air out overnight.

In the morning stir the starter thoroughly. Pour off 2 cups and set aside. Pour remaining 2 cups into glass jar, cover and return to refrigerator. Mix the ½ cup warm water, 1 teaspoon sugar, ½ teaspoon ginger and 1 package dry yeast. Set in warm place until foaming nicely. Heat the 1½ cups apricot nectar and dissolve the lemon gelatin in it. Cool to just warm. Pour the 2 cups reserved starter into mixing bowl. Add the warm apricot juice and gelatin, 1 cup dried skim milk and 3 cups white flour. Beat thoroughly. Add the dry yeast mixture and beat again. Add ½ cup soft butter, 1½ teaspoons salt and 2½ cups white flour. Stir until the dough clears the bowl. Spread remaining 1 cup flour on pastry board. Turn out dough, knead thoroughly using only enough flour to make a smooth non-sticky dough. Return to bowl, brush top of dough with butter, cover and set in warm place to rise. When light (this dough rises very quickly) turn out dough and knead lightly. Divide and shape as desired. Place in buttered pans, brush tops with butter and let rise until light. Bake in oven preheated to 350 degrees about 45 minutes for loaves and 25 for rolls. This recipe will make 4 high, well-rounded loaves. There are many ways to use this fragrant, yellow dough.

Fruit Loaf

2 cups Apricot Lemon dough
¾ cup finely chopped dried apricots

¾ cup puffed, seeded raisins
¾ cup chopped English walnuts or pecans

Pat out dough into thin rectangle. Sprinkle surface with apricots (use moist, tender ones; do not cook), seeded raisins and chopped walnuts or pecans. Roll up and then knead until fruit and nuts are well distributed throughout the dough. Shape into loaf and place in buttered pan. Spread top of loaf generously with butter. Let rise until very light. Bake in oven preheated to 400°F. for 15 minutes, reduce heat to 350 degrees and continue baking for about 35 minutes. Brush top of loaf with cream or canned milk about 5 minutes before the end of the baking period.

Pink Party Bread

2 cups starter
1½ cups cold water
1½ cups white flour

½ cup warm water
1 teaspoon sugar
½ teaspoon ginger
1 package dry yeast
1½ cups cherry juice, or 1½ cups water and 2 teaspoons cherry flavoring

1 6-ounce box cherry-flavored gelatin
1 cup dried skim milk powder
3 cups white flour
½ cup soft butter
1½ teaspoons salt
3½ cups white flour

Empty starter from glass jar into large mixing bowl (do not use metal or plastic). Add 1½ cups water and 1½ cups flour. Beat thoroughly. Cover tightly (clinging transparent wrap is good) and set in warm place (about 80°F.) overnight. Wash and scald starter jar and lid. Allow to air out overnight.

In the morning stir the starter thoroughly. Pour off 2 cups and set aside. Pour the remaining 2 cups starter into glass jar; cover and return to refrigerator. Mix the ½ cup warm water,

1 teaspoon sugar, ½ teaspoon ginger and 1 package dry yeast. Set in warm place until foaming nicely. Heat the 1½ cups cherry juice or 1½ cups water and 2 teaspoons cherry flavoring. Dissolve in it 1 large box cherry flavor gelatin. Cool to just warm. Pour the 2 cups reserved starter into mixing bowl. Add the cooled cherry juice mixture, 1 cup dried skim milk and 3 cups white flour. Mix well. Add the dry yeast mixture and beat well. Add ½ cup soft butter, 1½ teaspoons salt and 2½ cups white flour. Stir until the mixture clears the bowl. Spread remaining 1 cup flour on the pastry board. Turn out dough and knead thoroughly using only enough flour to make a smooth, nonsticky dough. Return to bowl, brush top of dough with butter, cover and set in warm place to rise. When light (this dough rises very quickly) turn out dough and knead lightly. Divide and shape as desired. Place in buttered pans, let rise until light. Bake in oven preheated to 350 degrees for about 45 minutes for loaves and 25 minutes for rolls. This recipe makes 4 high well-rounded loaves, or 48 muffin rolls, or 4 8-inch fluted rings, or 4 11-inch long half-round loaves in nut-bread pans.

For a children's party, press a whole candied cherry well down into the center of each muffin roll. When light and ready for the oven press down lightly again so that the cherries will not pop out while baking. Do not allow crust to become too brown. Turn down oven to 325 degrees if necessary. Rolls in Teflon-coated pans brown more quickly than others. When rolls have cooled to just warm dribble powdered-sugar icing around cherries and let it drip down the sides. These rolls will have the texture of big puffy pink marshmallows inside the tender crust.

For a Washington's Birthday party cut the half-round loaves into thick slices and decorate to resemble Martha's fan.

For an afternoon tea make thin sandwiches from plain loaves with whipped butter or cream cheese. If a plain white bread and a yellow one, such as Apricot Lemon, are available from the freezer, make a tray of varicolored sandwiches.

For an evening buffet supper, ice the fluted rings and decorate with colors appropriate for the occasion to serve with fresh fruit marinated in May wine.

Spiced Peach Bread

2 cups starter
1½ cups cold water
1½ cups white flour

1½ cups syrup from commercial or home-canned spiced peaches
1 6-ounce box peach-flavored gelatin
½ cup warm water
1 teaspoon sugar

½ teaspoon ginger
1 package dry yeast
1 cup dried skim milk powder
3 cups white flour
½ teaspoon yellow food coloring (if desired)
½ cup soft butter
1½ teaspoon salt
3½ cups white flour

Empty starter from glass jar into large mixing bowl (do not use metal or plastic). Add 1½ cups cold water and 1½ cups white flour. Beat thoroughly. Cover tightly (clinging transparent wrap is good) and set in warm place (about 80°F.) overnight. Wash and scald starter jar and lid. Allow to air out overnight.

In the morning stir the starter thoroughly. Pour off 2 cups and set aside. Pour remaining 2 cups into glass jar, cover and return to refrigerator. Heat 1½ cups spiced peach syrup. Dissolve 1 large box peach gelatin in it and cool to just warm. Mix ½ cup warm water, 1 teaspoon sugar, ½ teaspoon ginger and 1 package dry yeast. Set in warm place until foaming nicely. Pour the 2 cups reserved starter into mixing bowl. Add the peach syrup and gelatin, 1 cup dried skim milk, 3 cups white flour and ½ teaspoon yellow coloring (the bread will have a rather dull cream color without it). Beat thoroughly. Add the dry yeast mixture as soon as ready and beat again. Add ½ cup soft butter, 1½ teaspoons salt and 2½ cups white flour. Stir until the dough clears the bowl. Spread the remaining 1 cup flour on pastry board. Turn out dough (it will be very soft) and knead thoroughly using a little more flour if necessary to make a smooth, nonsticky dough. Return to the bowl, brush top of dough with butter, cover and set in warm place to rise (this dough is rather slow so give it plenty of time). When light, turn out, knead well, divide and shape as desired. Place in buttered pans, brush tops with butter, cover and set in warm place until light. Bake in oven preheated to 350 degrees for about 45 minutes for loaves, 25 minutes for rolls. This recipe makes 4 high, well-rounded small loaves.

Double Coffee Round

Follow directions for Fruit Loaf* until dough is ready to shape. Divide in half and roll out into circles to fit 2 9-inch layer cake pans. Place in the buttered pans and pat out even. Brush tops generously with butter and sprinkle with sugar and mace or nutmeg. Let rise until very light. Bake in oven preheated to 350°F. for about 35 minutes. As soon as removed from oven, cover top of one round with marshmallows placed closely together. Sprinkle with coconut. Place under broiler or on top shelf of oven until marshmallows start to melt and coconut is lightly toasted. Watch carefully. Remove from oven and place second round on top immediately.

* See recipe page 109.

Peach Fruit Loaf

2½ cup portion Spiced Peach dough

½ cup finely slivered unblanched almonds

½ cup golden raisins

½ cup finely chopped dried peaches

12 green candied cherries, chopped

Flatten the dough, sprinkle with the nuts and fruit, roll up and knead until all are well distributed through the dough. Form into loaf, place in buttered pan, brush top with butter, cover and let rise until very light. Bake in oven preheated to 350°F. for 50 to 55 minutes. Turn heat down to 325° during the last of baking period if crust is browning more than desired. This makes 1 large loaf. This bread is so fragrant and flavorful that it is nice to make up the whole batch of dough into fruit loaves at holiday time, or any time of the year, to store in freezer.

Crisscross Center Rolls

1½ cup portion Spiced Peach dough

¾ cup white flour

½ cup white sugar

½ cup lard

¼ teaspoon salt

½ teaspoon mace

1 teaspoon almond flavoring

½ egg, well beaten

Mix the flour, sugar, lard (butter may be used), salt, mace and almond flavoring as for pie dough. Work in beaten egg until mixture is moistened enough to work with hands into a roll about as large as a dollar. Cut into 12 sections and reshape until perfectly round. Divide the dough into 12 pieces. Shape into balls. Lay on Teflon-coated or very lightly greased cookie sheet.

Brush tops with butter. With fingers make round depression in center of rolls leaving only a film of dough at the bottom. Place a round of filling in each depression. With a fork make criss-cross marks on filling. Let rise until very light. Bake slowly at 325°F. for about 30 minutes so that the puffy dough rings will not become too brown while the thick filling is baking thoroughly. The crisscross markings remain distinct and when just a lovely meringue-brown make a most unusual and attractive sweet roll.

West Coast French Sourdough Bread I

Quick Method

1 cup starter	1 package dry yeast
¾ cup flour	3 cups flour
¾ cup water	2 teaspoons salt
	½ teaspoon soda
1½ cups warm water	2 cups flour
2 teaspoons sugar	

About 9:00 in the evening measure out 1 cup starter from the refrigerator storage jar into mixing bowl (do not use metal or plastic). Add ¾ cup water and ¾ cup flour and beat thoroughly. Cover bowl tightly with clinging transparent wrap and set in warm place (80 to 85°F.) overnight.

In the morning about 7:00 beat starter thoroughly. Measure out 1 cup and return remaining starter to storage jar. In another bowl pour 1½ cups of just warm water, stir in 2 teaspoons sugar and sprinkle 1 package dry yeast on top. Let stand until yeast is dissolved. Add the 1 cup of reserved starter and 3 cups flour. Beat thoroughly, cover tightly and let stand in warm place until very light and foamy. This will take from 1 to 1½ hours.*

Sift 2 teaspoons salt and ½ teaspoon soda with 1 cup flour and spread the remaining 1 cup on the pastry board. Stir the sifted flour mix into the sponge. Turn out on board and knead for several minutes using a little more flour if necessary to make a very stiff dough. Knead until completely smooth and non-sticky so that it can be worked on an unfloured portion of the board without sticking. Divide in halves and shape into either round or long narrow loaves. Place on flat baking sheet, preferably Teflon-coated but if one is not available, lightly grease it or sprinkle corn meal over the surface. Slip into large plastic bag, supported so that it will not touch dough (drinking glasses placed at each end of sheet are fine). Set in warm place for 1 to 1½ hours to rise.

If the dough becomes too light the loaves will spread in baking but this only makes a more delicious crust. When ready for the oven brush top of loaves with cold water. Make diagonal slashes across top of long loaves and five or six radiating from center of round ones with a sharp single-edge razor blade or scissors. Bake in oven preheated to 400 degrees with pan of hot water on the floor from 50 to 60 minutes and the crust is as dark as desired. About 10 minutes before the end of the baking period brush tops with water again. Remove from pans and stand on edge to cool, propping them against a heavy glass jar or similar object.

For the most attractive slices, especially if the loaves have spread a little too much in baking, cut with a very sharp knife diagonally across the long loaf and at the same time have the blade slanted from top to bottom away from the end. This makes

---

*For the really sour taste traditional in San Francisco sourdough bread, let this mixture stand for an additional 18–36 hours. The dough will be pungent, to say the least, but don't throw it out.

the slices about twice as wide as when cut straight up and down. Cut slices from the round loaves on the slant also. When ready to serve, to preserve the utterly delicious taste and crisp, hard crust, re-heat quickly with wrapping open at one end so that the bread will not become steamy, or spread slices with butter and place under broiler at high heat for a very short period until the edges are beginning to brown nicely. This recipe makes 2 long or 2 large round loaves which will just fit on a 12 x 15 inch baking sheet.

West Coast French Sourdough Bread II

Slow Method

Proceed as for Quick Method except omit the 1 package dry yeast. It will take at least 2½ hours for the first rising period and the sponge will not appear as light and puffy as with the yeast. Then it will take at least 2 hours for the loaves to become light after shaping. This method will result in a finer, more chewy texture, more pungent taste and aroma and a wonderful toasty, hard crust which will crumble more when sliced, but don't waste even a speck of it. Add the crumbs to breakfast cereal or use to top baked casserale dishes, etc.

Any sourdough bread is even more appealing when made with natural unbleached flour. If any adjustment is necessary in the amount of flour make it in the final portion before shaping loaves. Also, the older the starter you use, the better will be the taste and aroma in sourdough bread.

It seems almost impossible that such a "lean" list of ingredients could make such delicious bread but it does!

4
Cooked Potato Starter in Home Baking

Cooked Potato Starter

First prepare the following ferment:

4 tablespoons corn meal   1½ teaspoons salt
  (white or yellow)   1 cup milk
2 tablespoons sugar

Mix the corn meal, sugar and salt with the cold milk until smooth and free from lumps (use fresh or homogenized milk). Heat to the scalding point, stirring constantly. While still hot pour into an enameled or stoneware container which can be covered tightly. Keep in a comfortably warm place (about 80°F.) until the mush ferments and becomes quite light. This will take about four days in winter, but perhaps only two in warm, humid weather.

Stir the mush at least once a day. At first the liquid will separate and rise to the top. Then, as the fermentation proceeds, the settlings will rise up through the liquid until the whole mixture is uniformly spongy and the bubbles can be seen working to the top. When the ferment has reached this stage prepare the following:

3 medium-size potatoes	3 tablespoons sugar
1 quart water	2 teaspoons salt

Cook the potatoes in the water until tender. Drain off the water. If too much has boiled away add more water to make 3 cups of liquid. Put potatoes through food mill or sieve, then combine with the 3 cups of liquid, sugar and salt. When this mixture has cooled to comfortably warm, stir in the ferment. This should be done early in the day as the mixture should now stand in a warm place for several hours. Stir it down each time it becomes foamy. Then store in a covered 2-quart glass jar in the refrigerator for 2 to 3 days to ripen before using. Stir or shake until thoroughly mixed each time before removing a portion of the starter. When the amount has been reduced to about 1 to 1½ cups add this to a newly prepared mixture of potatoes, potato water, sugar and salt and proceed as before.

Saint Nicholas Bread

Late in the evening (about 9:00) make a sponge of the following:

2 cups warm water	3 tablespoons sugar or
4 cups natural, unbleached	white corn syrup
stone-ground white flour*	1½ cups starter

Beat together thoroughly, cover tightly in a large mixing bowl and let stand in comfortably warm place overnight. Early in the morning (about 7:00) make a dough with the following ingredients:

---
* See Sources of Supply.

2 cups warm water
1 cup dried skim milk
powder
½ teaspoon ginger

6 tablespoons soft lard
3 tablespoons sugar
3 teaspoons salt
9 cups natural flour

Stir the dried milk and ginger into the warm water. Add to the sponge with the other ingredients, reserving 2 cups of the flour to spread on the pastry board. Stir until the dough clears the bowl. Turn out onto the floured board and knead thoroughly for several minutes, using a little more flour if necessary to make a smooth, nonsticky dough. Return to bowl, brush top with lard, cover with a light towel and let rise until light (about 8:30). Turn out dough, knead well without using any more flour than necessary, divide and shape into loaves or rolls as desired. Place in greased pans, brush tops with soft lard, cover and let rise until the pans feel quite light when lifted (about 10:30). Bake in oven preheated to 350°F. about 30 minutes for rolls and 50 to 60 minutes for loaves, according to size. About 5 minutes before the end of the baking period brush top of bread with soft lard or butter and again as soon as removed from oven. Turn loaves on side to cool. This recipe makes 6 medium-size loaves.

For a coffee loaf which is delicious toasted, roll a loaf-size portion of dough into a long rectangle as wide as the length of the pan. Sprinkle with 2 tablespoons vanilla sugar mixed with ½ teaspoon instant coffee. Roll as for cinnamon rolls, but instead of cutting, roll into long rectangle again. Sprinkle with 2 tablespoons sugar mixed with ½ teaspoon cinnamon. Roll, seal ends and place seam-side down in pan. Proceed as with plain loaf for baking.

Note: Vanilla sugar can be purchased in sealed packets or can easily be prepared at home by simply keeping four or five vanilla beans buried in two cups sugar in a tightly closed glass jar. Replace the amount of sugar used each time until the beans become dry and begin to lose their aroma. They can be split and the seeds scraped out to mix with the sugar or boiled in milk to get the last bit of flavor when making custard, rice pudding, ice cream, etc.

Chestnut Bread

Late in the evening (about 9:00) make a sponge of the following:

2 cups chestnut purée   3 cups white flour
4 tablespoons sugar   1½ cups starter
1 cup warm water

Beat all ingredients together thoroughly in a large mixing bowl, cover tightly and let stand in a comfortably warm place overnight. Early in the morning (about 7:00) add the following:

1 cup warm water   3 teaspoons salt
1 cup dried skim milk   4 tablespoons sugar
   powder   4 tablespoons soft butter
½ teaspoon ginger   5 cups white flour

Stir the dried milk and ginger into the warm water. Add to the sponge with the salt, sugar, butter and 4 cups of the white flour. Stir until the dough clears the bowl (the chestnut purée is so dry it absorbs more moisture than vegetable purée so less flour is needed in proportion to the amount of liquid than in other recipes). Spread the remaining 1 cup of flour on the pastry board, turn out dough and knead thoroughly, using a little more flour if necessary, to make a smooth nonsticky dough. Return to bowl, brush top of dough with butter, cover and let rise until light. Turn out, knead well, using as little flour as possible, divide and shape into rolls or loaves as desired. Place in greased pans, brush tops with butter. Set in warm place to rise until pans feel quite light when lifted. Bake in oven preheated to 400°F. but turn the heat down to 350° as soon as the oven is closed. It will take about 30 minutes for rolls and 50 to 55 minutes for loaves, depending on size. This recipe will make 4 medium-size loaves.

This bread has such a rich, ripe taste and aroma with tender, crunchy crust that the dough is ideal for making up into almost any shape and kind of dessert bread such as fruit-filled coffee rings, cinnamon rolls, pinwheels, muffin rolls, and egg-glazed challahs to name just a few.

Note: To prepare the purée soak dried chestnuts overnight in warm water. Boil them in the same water until tender. Drain and put through food mill. One pound of shelled dry nuts will make about 5 cups of purée. This can be stored in freezer for future baking or used in many other ways such as delicious desserts, candy, dressings for fowl, and soups.

Chili-Bean Bread

Late in the evening (about 9:00) make a sponge of the following:

2 cups warm water	2 cups white flour
2 cups cooked, sieved navy beans	3 tablespoons brown sugar
	1½ cups starter

Beat together thoroughly, cover tightly in a large mixing bowl and let stand in comfortably warm place overnight. Early in the morning (about 7:00) make a dough with the following ingredients:

2 cups warm water
1 cup dried skim milk
   powder
½ teaspoon ginger
6 tablespoons soft shortening

2 teaspoons salt
3 tablespoons brown sugar
3 teaspoons chili powder
7 cups white flour

Stir the dried milk and ginger into the warm water. Add to the sponge together with the shortening, salt, brown sugar, chili powder and 5 cups of the white flour. Stir until the dough clears the bowl. Spread the remaining 2 cups of white flour on the pastry board, turn out dough and knead thoroughly for several minutes, using a little more flour if necessary to make a smooth, nonsticky dough. Return to bowl, grease top of dough and let rise until light (about 9:00). Turn out, knead well without using any more flour than necessary. Divide and shape into loaves, hamburger buns or hot dog rolls. Place in greased pans, butter tops, cover with thin towel or Saran wrap. Let rise until the pans feel quite light when lifted (about 11:00). Bake in oven preheated to 350°F., 30 minutes for rolls and buns, 50 minutes for medium-sized loaves. This dough makes superlative buns light as a feather, tender and as soft in texture as sponge-cake. The amount of chili powder used gives a very mild flavor and a most appetizing aroma. More could be used if one is especially fond of it.

Note: To prepare the beans, heat 1 pound of Great Northern to the boiling point in water to cover, stir in ½ teaspoon baking soda, drain and rinse. Simmer in a small amount of unsalted water until tender and mealy. Drain and put enough through a food mill or sieve to make 2 cups.

Spiced Rye Bread

Late in the evening (about 9:00) make a sponge of the following:

2 cups warm water	1 cup old-fashioned, coarse
3 tablespoons molasses	oatmeal
3 cups rye flour	1½ cups starter

Beat together thoroughly, cover tightly in a large mixing bowl, and let stand in a comfortably warm place overnight. Early in the morning (about 7:00) add the following ingredients:

2 cups warm water	3 tablespoons molasses
1 cup dried skim milk powder	3 tablespoons crushed, whole allspice
½ teaspoon ginger	3 tablespoons dehydrated pulverized orange rind
2 teaspoons salt	
6 tablespoons soft butter	8 cups white flour

Stir the dried milk and ginger into the warm water. Add to the sponge with the other ingredients, reserving 3 cups of the white flour to spread on the pastry board. Turn out the dough and knead thoroughly. When enough flour has been worked in to make it firm, mound up dough into a ball, cover with inverted bowl or cloth and let rest for 10 to 20 minutes. Knead again working in more flour if necessary to make a good stiff dough (this bread rises very light with a rather coarse texture so it will not hold up unless the dough is stiff). Return to bowl, brush top with butter, cover and let rise until light (about 9:00). Turn out, knead, divide and shape into loaves or buns as desired. Place in greased pans, brush tops with butter, let rise until pans feel quite light when lifted (about 11:00). Bake in oven preheated to 350°F. for about 1 hour for loaves and 30 minutes for large buns. About 10 minutes before the end of the baking period, brush tops of bread with evaporated milk. If the buns are to be used as soon as cool it is very nice to add a little sugar and cinnamon to the milk for a spicy glaze. If they are to be stored in freezer, wait until they are reheated to add the glaze. This recipe will make 4 medium loaves and 15 buns.

Scotch Oatmeal Bread

Late in the evening (about 9:00) make a sponge of the following:

2 cups Scotch oatmeal	3 tablespoons brown sugar
(cracked whole-grain oats)	2 cups white flour
2 cups boiling water	1½ cups starter

Pour the boiling water over the cracked oats and let stand until just comfortably warm to the hand. Add the remaining ingredients, stir well, cover tightly and let stand in a warm place overnight. Early in the morning (about 7:00) make a dough with the following ingredients:

2 cups warm water	6 tablespoons maple-flavored
1 cup dried skim milk	syrup
powder	6 tablespoons soft butter
½ teaspoon ginger	6 cups white flour
2 teaspoons salt	

Stir the dried milk and ginger into the warm water. Add to the sponge together with the salt, butter, syrup and 4 cups of the white flour. Stir until the dough clears the bowl. Spread the remaining 2 cups of white flour on the pastry board, turn out the dough and knead thoroughly for several minutes, using a little more flour if necessary to make a fairly firm, nonsticky dough. Return to bowl, brush top of dough with butter, cover and let rise until light (about 9:00). Turn out, knead well without using any more flour than necessary, divide and shape into loaves or rolls as desired. Brush tops with butter, cover and set in warm place to rise until the pans feel quite light when lifted. Bake in oven preheated to 350°F. about 30 minutes for rolls and 1 hour for loaves. This recipe makes 5 high, well-rounded loaves in medium-size pans. About 5 minutes before the end of the baking period brush tops of loaves with butter again.

The plain loaves make a marvelous toast with rich, nutlike flavor but, for an even more delicious toast or just fresh faintly warm slices to serve with butter make a Raisin Log by rolling out a loaf-size portion of dough into a long rectangle as wide as the loaf pan is long. Stud it thickly with puffed seeded raisins and, if you like a distinct maple flavor, sprinkle just a very few drops of the flavoring over the dough. Add a dusting of cinnamon too, if you like. Roll up, place in greased pan with seam-side down and proceed as with the plain loaves.

Gossip Tea Bread

About 7:00 in the evening pour 2 cups boiling water over 4 bags of Gossip Tea and 16 whole cloves. Cover tightly and let stand for 2 hours. Remove bags and cloves. About 9:00 make a sponge with

2 cups warm Gossip Tea	4 tablespoons honey
4 cups white flour	1½ cups starter

Beat all together thoroughly, cover tightly in a large mixing bowl and let stand in comfortably warm place overnight. Early in the morning (about 7:00) make a dough with the following ingredients:

1 cup dried skim milk powder	3 teaspoons salt
½ teaspoon ginger	4 tablespoons honey
2 cups warm water	6 tablespoons soft butter
3 whole eggs, well beaten with 3 extra egg yolks	8 cups white flour

Stir the dried milk and ginger into the warm water. Add to the sponge together with the beaten eggs, salt, honey, butter and 6 cups of the white flour. Stir until the dough clears the bowl. Spread the remaining 2 cups of flour on the pastry board, turn out dough and knead thoroughly for several minutes working in enough flour to make a smooth, nonsticky dough. Return to the bowl, brush top of dough with butter, cover and let rise until light (about 9:00). Turn out, knead well without using any more flour than necessary, divide and shape into rolls or loaves as desired. Place in greased pans, brush tops with butter, cover with cloth and set in warm place to rise until pans feel quite light when lifted. Bake in oven preheated to 350°F. about 30 minutes for rolls and 1 hour for loaves. About 5 minutes before the end of the baking period brush top of bread with soft butter again, or with evaporated milk for a glossy crust. This recipe makes 5 medium-size loaves.

Note: Gossip Tea, sold under the brand name of Colonial Gossip Tea, contains no real tea. "Gossip" was a name given to herb teas in Colonial days because the women talked so much while drinking it. If using the natural blend tea which contains only crushed Rose Hips, Roselle Seeds, cloves and dried orange rind, I empty the contents of the soaked bags into the tea. This gives an interesting speckled effect to the dough besides adding a little more vitamin C. Alfalfa tea is also excellent to use (without the cloves) in making this bread.

Parsnip Bread

Late in the evening (about 9:00) make a sponge of the following:

2 cups drained, sieved parsnips
3 tablespoons white corn syrup

1 cup warm water
3 cups white flour
1½ cups starter

Steam 5 to 6 large parsnips in a small amount of water until tender. Drain well, put through food mill or sieve. Cool until just warm. Beat all together thoroughly in a large mixing bowl, cover tightly and let stand in comfortably warm place overnight. Early in the morning (about 7:00) make a dough with the following ingredients:

1 cup warm water
1 cup dried skim milk powder
½ teaspoon ginger
2 teaspoons salt

6 tablespoons soft butter
3 tablespoons white corn syrup
6 cups white flour

Stir the dried milk and ginger into the warm water. Add to the sponge with the salt, butter, syrup and 4 cups of the white flour. Stir well until the dough clears the bowl (a little more flour may be necessary, depending on how much moisture the parsnips retained). Spread the remaining amount of white flour on the pastry board, turn out dough and knead thoroughly for several minutes, using a little more flour if needed to make a smooth, nonsticky dough. Return to the bowl, brush top of dough with butter, cover and let rise until light. Turn out, knead well, using as little flour as possible, divide and shape into loaves or rolls as desired. Place in greased pans, brush tops with butter, and set in warm place to rise until pans feel quite light when lifted. Bake in oven preheated to 400°F., then turn down to 350° as soon as bread is in oven. It will take about 30 minutes for rolls and 50 to 60 minutes for loaves. This recipe makes 4 medium-size loaves.

Turnips, white potatoes, sweet potatoes, squash and pumpkin all can be used equally well in place of the parsnips. The other ingredients may all be left the same, but I like to use white sugar and lard with turnips and potatoes, brown sugar and peanut oil with sweet potatoes, maple-flavored syrup with squash and pumpkin and occasionally add a combination of other spices with the ginger for variety.

Soy and Sorghum Bread

Late in the evening (about 9:00) make a sponge of the following:

2 cups warm water	3 tablespoons sugar
4 cups white flour	1½ cups starter

Beat all together thoroughly, cover tightly in large mixing bowl and let stand in comfortably warm place overnight. Early in the morning (about 7:00) make a dough with the following ingredients:

2 cups scalded and cooled milk	6 tablespoons soft margarine (or corn or peanut oil)
1 teaspoon ginger	4 cups *sifted* soy flour*
3 tablespoons sorghum	3 cups white flour
3 teaspoons salt	

* See Sources of Supply.

Stir ginger into the cooled milk and add to the sponge with the other ingredients, reserving 2 cups of the white flour to spread on the pastry board. Stir until the dough clears the bowl. Turn out on board and knead thoroughly for several minutes working in enough of the flour to make a smooth, nonsticky dough. Return to bowl, grease top of dough, cover and let rise until about 9:30. Since the soy flour is quite heavy and fine the dough will not be as light and spongy as an all white flour dough would be. However, turn it out, knead well again and divide. Shape into loaves, place in greased pans, brush tops with margarine or butter, cover and set in warm place to rise. This will take a longer period of time because of the soy flour but wait until loaves which half filled the pans almost reach the top rim. Have oven preheated to 400°F. As soon as loaves are set in, reduce to 350° and bake about 45 minutes for small loaves and 1 hour for medium loaves. I prefer to bake this bread in the small pans because it holds up better and also because the crust is so delicious, especially when toasted. I like to expose as much dough as possible to surface baking. This recipe will make 6 small loaves. All that is not to be used within a day or two should be wrapped and stored in freezer or refrigerator as soon as the bread is cooled.

Be sure to sift the soy flour. Because of its nature it has a tendency to pack and become lumpy in the sack. Some brands seem to absorb more moisture than others. The salt may be omitted for a salt free diet.

Snap, Crackle, Pop Bread

Late in the evening (about 9:00) make a sponge of the following:

2 cups uncooked cracked
   wheat
2 cups boiling water

4 tablespoons honey
2 cups white flour
1½ cups starter

Pour the boiling water over the cracked wheat and let stand until just warm to the hand. Add the remaining ingredients, beat well, cover tightly and let stand in a warm place overnight. Early in the morning (about 7:00) make a dough with the following ingredients:

2 cups warm water
1 cup dried skim milk
   powder
½ teaspoon ginger

2 teaspoons salt
6 tablespoons soft butter
4 tablespoons honey
6 cups white flour

Stir the dried milk and ginger into the warm water. Add to the sponge together with the salt, butter, honey and 4 cups of white flour. Stir until the dough clears the bowl. Spread the remaining 2 cups white flour on the pastry board, turn out dough and knead thoroughly for several minutes, using as much flour as necessary to make a smooth, nonsticky dough. Return to the bowl, brush top of dough with butter, cover and let rise in warm place until light. Turn out, knead well without using any more flour than necessary, divide and shape into loaves or rolls as desired. Place in greased pans, brush tops with butter, and set in warm place to rise until the pans feel quite light when lifted. Bake in oven preheated to 350°F. about 30 minutes for rolls and 50 to 55 minutes for loaves. About 5 minutes before the end of the baking period brush top of bread with butter or evaporated milk. This recipe makes 6 medium-size loaves.

When slices of this bread are put in the toaster they will snap, crackle and pop as loudly as the best talking cereal. The test of a good loaf of bread is the kind of toast it makes and this one passes that test with a high score.

5

Interchangeable Starters

and Ways to Use Them

Peach Leaf Dry Yeast starter and Dry Yeast Starter can be interchanged with Grated Raw Potato Starter (Chapter 3).

Peach Leaf Starter, Beer Starter, English Ginger Beer Starter and Hop Starter can all be used in the recipes in this chapter.

Peach Leaf Starter

1 quart fresh peach leaves, un- 	½ cup yellow corn meal
  packed 	3 tablespoons sugar
3 cups water 	2 teaspoons salt
3 baked potatoes, medium size

Bring water to rolling boil and steep peach leaves in it for 15 minutes. Drain liquid and add enough water to make 3 full cups again. This will have a rather unappetizing green color but don't worry! It will disappear during the fermentation process. Peel hot baked potatoes and put through food mill or sieve. Scald ½ cup corn meal in 1 cup of the liquid until it reaches boiling point and thickens. Stir constantly so that it will not become lumpy. Now combine all ingredients in large mixing bowl (do not use metal or plastic). Cover with cheesecloth and set in warm place (about 80 to 85°F.) until well fermented. In warm humid weather this will take about 24 hours. In cool dry weather a few more hours may be required for mixture to become active throughout. Stir every few hours during the process. When it is ready, pour into a large glass jar (I use a 2-quart glass pickle jar with porcelain-lined zinc lid). Store in refrigerator at about 38 degrees. If necessary stir down a time or two until it stops foaming. It is ready for use when about ½ inch of clear liquid has risen to the top. This will take about 2 days. Stir well each time before using.

When this starter has been used down to about 1 cupful, add 3 cups water, 3 medium-size baked potatoes, ½ cup corn meal scalded in 1 cup of the water, 3 tablespoons sugar and 2 teaspoons salt prepared as for the first time (peach leaves are not needed after the first time). Set in warm place until it becomes very active in about 6 to 8 hours. Store in refrigerator and it will be ready for use the next day. A properly renewed starter improves with age and, once one becomes accustomed to taking care of it, it all becomes automatic. When, for some reason, it cannot be used about twice a week stir it thoroughly every few days and add 1 teaspoon sugar. Each time it is renewed, empty the jar, wash and scald jar and lid before filling with the new mixture.

Peach Leaf Dry Yeast

Follow directions for making Peach Leaf Starter until it is ready to store in refrigerator. Sterilize about 2 quarts of corn meal for 1 hour in oven, at low temperature so that it will not brown. Stir often. After it has cooled stir as much of this into the fermented mixture as it will absorb. Spread ½ inch thick in flat pans. When it has set enough, cut into 1½-inch squares. Separate and lay on clean towels or absorbent paper to dry. Do not place in the sun. Be careful that insects do not have access to it during the drying process. When completely dry and hard, wrap each cake in small squares of cellophane and seal with tape. Store in refrigerator in moistureproof container. This will keep for a year or more.

Only a portion of the starter mixture may be taken to make a small number of cakes if desired. Then only a proportionate amount of corn meal need be sterilized.

A Starter from Dry Yeast

When fresh peach leaves are not available, a starter can be made by combining 1 cake Peach Leaf Dry Yeast, ½ cup warm water, ½ teaspoon ginger and 1 teaspoon sugar in glass bowl. Cover with cheesecloth and let stand in warm place (80 to 85°F.) until a white film covers the top of the water. This will only take overnight in warm, humid weather, a little longer in cool weather. Add ½ cup water (room temperature), ½ cup white flour and 1 teaspoon sugar. Stir well, cover and let stand until foamy. Again add ½ cup water (room temperature), 1 cup white flour and 1 teaspoon sugar. Let stand until foaming actively. Stir often. Pour into glass fruit jar and store in refrigerator with lid loose until foaming has stopped. As soon as about ½ inch of clear liquid has risen to the top the starter has ripened enough to use.

Beer Starter

3 medium potatoes	2 teaspoons salt
3 cups water	Foam from 12-ounce can
½ cup corn meal	chilled beer
3 tablespoons sugar	

Cook the potatoes in the water until tender. Drain off liquid and add more water if necessary to make 3 full cups again. Put potatoes through food mill or sieve. Scald the corn meal in 1 cup of the potato water until it reaches the boiling point and thickens, stirring constantly to be sure that no lumps form. Now combine the sieved potatoes, 2 cups potato water, corn meal mixture, sugar and salt in large bowl (do not use metal or plastic). Let cool until just warm. Pour the cold beer slowly into a large glass. Immediately skim off all the foam and stir into the mixture in the bowl. Cover tightly (clinging transparent wrap is good) and set in warm place (80 to 85°F.) until fermentation is complete. In warm, humid weather this will take about 24 hours. In cold weather it may require several more hours for the starter to become foamy throughout. Stir occasionally during the process. Pour into a large (about 2-quart size) glass container and store in the refrigerator at about 38 degrees. Do not put the lid on tightly until the working has subsided.

Let starter ripen about 3 days until ½ inch or more of clear liquid has risen to the top. Stir thoroughly each time before a portion is removed for baking. When the supply has been reduced to about 1 cupful or a little more, repeat the beginning process with the exception that no more beer foam needs to be used. When the mixture of potatoes, potato water, corn meal mixture, salt and sugar are well blended and cool, add the remainder of the old starter and stir well. Cover and set in warm place until fermented as before (it should now take only 8 to 12 hours for this process). Store in refrigerator and let ripen again until the clear liquid comes to the top before starting to use from this new supply.

English Ginger Beer Starter

Using the recipe for Beer Starter, substitute ½ cup English Ginger Beer (found in either brown glass bottles or tin cans in the gourmet sections of most supermarkets) for the foam from chilled beer. This makes the very best-smelling starter I have ever worked with.

Hop Starter

1 quart loose hops*	½ cup yellow corn meal
3 cups water	3 tablespoons sugar
3 medium-size baked potatoes	2 teaspoons salt

Bring 3 cups water to rolling boil. Steep hops in it for 15 minutes. Drain liquid and add enough water to make 3 full cups again. Peel baked potatoes and put through fine sieve or food mill. Scald ½ cup yellow corn meal in 1 cup of the liquid just until it thickens, stirring constantly to prevent lumps. Combine all ingredients in large mixing bowl (do not use metal or plastic). When the mixture has cooled to just warm cover with cheesecloth and set in warm place (80 to 85°F.) until well fermented. In warm humid weather this will take about 24 hours. In cold, dry weather it may take 30 hours or a little more. Stir every few hours during the process. When it is foaming nicely throughout pour into a large glass jar (I use a 2-quart glass pickle jar with porcelain-lined zinc lid). Store in refrigerator at about 38 degrees. If necessary, stir down a time or two until it stops foaming. It is ready for use when about ½ inch of clear liquid has risen to the top in about 2 days.

When this starter has been used down to about 1 cupful, add 3 cups water, 3 medium-sized baked potatoes, ½ cup corn meal, 3 tablespoons sugar and 2 teaspoons salt prepared as for the first time. Set in warm place until it becomes very active in about 6 to 8 hours. Store in refrigerator and it will be ready for use the next day.

A properly renewed starter improves with age and once one

---

* See Sources of Supply.

becomes accustomed to taking care of it, it all becomes automatic. When for some reason it cannot be used about twice a week, stir it thoroughly every few days and add 1 teaspoon sugar. Each time it is renewed, empty the jar, wash and scald jar and lid before filling with the new mixture.

Everyday White Bread

1 cup starter	1 cup white flour
1½ cups white flour	½ teaspoon baking soda
2 cups cold water	½ teaspoon cream of tartar
¼ to ½ cup sugar	1 teaspoon salt
½ teaspoon ginger	¼ to ½ cup soft lard
1 cup dried skim milk powder	5 cups white flour

About 7:00 in the evening stir 1 cup starter and 1½ cups white flour together in mixing bowl (do not use metal or plastic) until a soft ball is formed. Let stand uncovered for 2 hours. Stir the sugar (¼ cup is enough to make good bread and is preferred by those who wish to limit sugar in their diet) and ½ teaspoon ginger into 2 cups cold water and pour over the ball of starter. Cover bowl tightly (clinging transparent wrap is good) and set in warm place (about 80°F.) overnight.

In the morning the ball of starter will have become foamy and risen to the top of the water. Beat thoroughly. Add 1 cup dried milk and 1 cup white flour sifted with ½ teaspoon baking soda, ½ teaspoon cream of tartar and 1 teaspoon salt. Beat thoroughly. Add the soft lard (½ cup makes a softer, richer texture) and 4 cups white flour. Stir until the dough clears the bowl. Spread the remaining 1 cup flour on the pastry board. Turn out dough and knead well, using a little more flour if necessary to make a smooth, nonsticky dough. Cover with cloth and let rest about 20 minutes. Divide and shape as desired. Place in well-greased or Teflon-coated pans. Brush tops with soft lard or butter. Cover and let rise in warm place until about double in bulk. Bake in oven preheated to 350 degrees for about 1 hour for large loaves. This recipe makes 2 large loaves.

Two favorite shapes for these loaves are the Twin Roll, and the Pull-apart. For the Twin Roll divide loaf-size portion in halves and make each into a roll as long as the pan. Place side by side in pan and brush generously with shortening so that division will remain. For the Pull-apart divide loaf-size portion of dough into even number of pieces of the size for small rolls. Make into balls, dip in melted butter and press tightly together in two rows in pan for a large loaf, one row for a small loaf. When baked each section will not be much thicker than a slice of bread and they can easily be separated with a fork to serve before the bread would be cool enough to slice. These sections, toasted quickly under the broiler are especially good to serve with homemade vegetable soup and rosy baked apples for lunch on a cold, rainy day.

If baking for a person who cannot have salt, omit it from the dough. Bake part of it this way and for the rest, sprinkle the greased sides and bottoms of the pans lightly with salt before placing the loaves in them. Also sprinkle top of loaves. They will be even more attractive if coarse salt crystals such as are used for salt sticks are available for this.

Graham Health Bread

1 cup starter
1½ cups white flour
2 cups cold water
¼ to ½ cup dark brown
    raw sugar*
½ teaspoon ginger
1 cup white flour
½ teaspoon baking soda

½ teaspoon cream of tartar
1 cup dried skim milk
    powder
¼ to ½ cup safflower oil
1½ teaspoons salt
5 cups stone-ground graham
    flour*

About 7:00 in the evening stir the 1 cup starter and 1½ cups white flour together in mixing bowl (do not use metal or plastic) until it forms a ball. Let stand uncovered for 2 hours. Stir the brown sugar (¼ cup gives no sweet taste but is sufficient to make good bread) and ½ teaspoon ginger into the 2 cups cold water. Pour over ball of starter in bowl. Cover tightly (clinging transparent wrap is good) and set in warm place (about 80°F.) overnight.

In the morning the ball of starter will have become foamy and risen to the top of the water. Beat thoroughly. Add the 1 cup white flour sifted with ½ teaspoon each of baking soda and cream of tartar. Beat well. Add 1 cup dried skim milk, safflower oil (the larger amount gives a more tender crust), 1½ teaspoons salt and 4 cups graham flour. Stir until the dough clears the bowl. Spread the remaining 1 cup graham flour on the pastry board. Turn out dough and knead thoroughly using a little more flour if necessary for a smooth nonsticky dough. Cover with light cloth and let rest for about 20 minutes. Divide and shape as desired. Place in greased pans, brush tops with oil, cover and let set in warm place to rise until dent remains when

* See Sources of Supply.

dough is pushed lightly with finger. Bake in oven preheated to 375 degrees for about 45 minutes for small loaves. If desired brush tops of loaves with cream or canned milk about 5 minutes before the end of the baking period. This recipe makes 4 high, well-rounded small loaves.

This bread is perfect for making delicious Dutch Crumb Cookies (see p. 169 for recipe). I always slice, toast and grind one loaf before storing in the freezer so that the crumbs are ready to use whenever needed. Regular brown sugar and other cooking oils can be substituted for the raw sugar and safflower oil if they are not available.

Rye Crumb Bread

1 cup starter
1½ cups white flour
2 cups cold water
4 tablespoons sorghum
½ teaspoon ginger
2 cups toasted, ground, rye
   bread crumbs
1 cup warm water
2 cups rye flour

2 tablespoons rice polish*
½ teaspoon baking soda
½ teaspoon cream of tartar
2 teaspoons instant coffee
4 tablespoons bacon
   drippings
1 teaspoon salt
3 cups white flour

About 7:00 in the evening stir 1 cup starter and 1½ cups white flour together in mixing bowl (do not use metal or plastic) until a soft ball is formed. Let stand uncovered for 2 hours. Stir the 2 cups cold water, 4 tablespoons sorghum and ½ teaspoon ginger together. Pour over the ball of starter. Sprinkle 2 cups rye bread crumbs over the top. Cover bowl tightly (clinging transparent wrap is good) and set in warm place (about 80°F.) overnight.

In the morning the starter will have become foamy and risen

---

* See Sources of Supply.

to the top. Beat thoroughly. Add 1 cup warm water and 2 cups rye flour sifted with 2 tablespoons rice polish, ½ teaspoon each of baking soda and cream of tartar and 2 teaspoons instant coffee. Beat well. Add 4 tablespoons melted bacon drippings, 1 teaspoon salt and 1 cup white flour. Stir until the dough clears the bowl. Spread a second 1 cup white flour on pastry board. Turn out dough and knead for several minutes working in all the flour. Form into ball, cover with mixing bowl and let rest for 20 minutes. Work as much of the third 1 cup white flour into the dough as possible. Divide and shape as desired. Place in greased pans, sprinkle tops heavily with flour. Cover with light cloth and set in warm place to rise. When ready for the oven brush tops of loaves with cold water or wine. Bake in oven preheated to 400 degrees for 15 minutes, reduce heat to 350 degrees and continue baking about 40 minutes longer. Brush tops with water or wine again about 5 minutes before end of baking period. This recipe makes 3 5-inch round loaves.

Note: For the first baking, crumbs of any other rye bread can be used, even those from commercially baked bread. Then prepared crumbs from this bread can be stored in freezer for use at any time.

Louisiana Yam Bread

1 cup starter	3 cups white flour
1½ cups flour	½ teaspoon baking soda
2 cups cold water	½ teaspoon cream of tartar
½ cup sugar	1 teaspoon nutmeg
1 teaspoon ginger	3 eggs, well-beaten
½ package (5 oz. size) instant yams	1½ teaspoons salt
1 cup dried skim milk powder	½ cup soft butter or margarine
	3 cups white flour

About 7:00 in the evening stir 1 cup starter and 1½ cups white flour together in mixing bowl (do not use metal or plastic) until it forms a soft ball. Let stand uncovered for 2 hours. Stir ½ cup sugar and 1 teaspoon ginger into 2 cups cold water. Pour over starter ball in bowl. Cover tightly (clinging transparent wrap is good) and set in warm place overnight (about 80°F.).

In the morning the ball of starter will have become foamy and risen to the top of the water. Beat thoroughly. Add ½ package yams, 1 cup dried skim milk and 3 cups white flour sifted with ½ teaspoon each baking soda and cream of tartar and 1 teaspoon nutmeg. Beat until well mixed. Add 3 well-beaten eggs, 1½ teaspoons salt, ½ cup shortening and 2 cups white flour. Stir until the dough clears the bowl. Spread remaining 1 cup white flour on pastry board. Turn out dough and knead thoroughly using a little more flour if necessary but the dough should be kept as soft as possible and still handle easily. Cover with a light cloth and let rest for about 20 minutes. Prepare the pans by buttering lightly. Divide dough and shape as desired. Place in pans, butter tops and set in warm place until light. Bake in oven preheated to 400 degrees for 15 minutes. Reduce heat to 350 degrees and continue baking about 40 minutes longer. Brush tops with cream or canned milk about 5 minutes before the end of the baking period for an extra tender crust. This recipe makes 3 high, well-rounded loaves.

This is one of those breads which cannot be left alone! The baker just has to sample a little end slice as soon as cool enough to cut, and then will not be able to resist going back for more. There is just enough spice to provide a faint aroma and only a hint of taste. With its beautiful rich, golden crust it is a perfect bread for any menu containing turkey, chicken or baked ham.

Note: Yams have high nutritional value, surpassing the white potato in proteins, sugars, fats and vitamins, especially vitamin A. This new instant product makes a lighter, drier, finer-textured bread than can be achieved with either canned or freshly cooked yams. (I use Royal Prince brand.)

Cheese and Dressing Bread

1 cup starter
1½ cups white flour
1½ cups cold water
½ cup white corn syrup
½ teaspoon ginger
1 cup dried skim milk
   powder
3 cups white flour
½ teaspoon baking soda

½ teaspoon cream of tartar
½ cup salad dressing
½ cup maple syrup cheese*
   finely crumbled
1½ teaspoons salt
3½ cups white flour
⅓ cup sesame seed
1 egg white
1 teaspoon cold water

About 7:00 in the evening stir the 1 cup starter and 1½ cups white flour together in mixing bowl (do not use plastic or metal) until it forms a ball. Let stand uncovered 2 hours. Stir the 1½ cups cold water, ½ cup white corn syrup and ½ teaspoon ginger together and pour over starter ball. Cover tightly (clinging transparent wrap is good) and set in warm place (about 80°F.) overnight.

In the morning the ball of starter will have become foamy and risen to the top of the water. Beat thoroughly. Add 1 cup dried skim milk, 3 cups white flour sifted with ½ teaspoon each of baking soda and cream of tartar. Beat well again. Add ½ cup salad dressing, ½ cup finely crumbled maple syrup cheese, 1½ teaspoons salt and 2½ cups white flour. Stir until the dough clears the bowl.

---

* See Sources of Supply.

Spread the remaining 1 cup white flour on the pastry board. Turn out dough and knead thoroughly using a very little more flour if necessary. Cover with light cloth and let rest for 20 minutes. Divide and shape as desired. Place in buttered pans. Slip into large plastic bag so that top surface will not dry and let rise in warm place until very light. Beat 1 egg white with 1 teaspoon cold water until frothy. Brush tops generously with this mixture. Sprinkle with sesame seed. Bake in oven preheated to 350 degrees for about 45 minutes for loaves, 25 minutes for rolls. Turn down temperature to 325 degrees during the last part of baking period if crust is becoming too brown. Sesame seeds are most delicious when only lightly toasted. This recipe makes 4 high, well-rounded small loaves.

Note: I prefer spin-blended dressing which contains less oil for the cheese is very rich. If the maple syrup cheese cannot be obtained other soft, crumbly cheese may be used but the velvety, fragrant New England product, slightly sweetened with the syrup is just right for this bread with its hard crust and tender, spongy texture.

Oat Groats Bread

1 cup starter	1 cup white flour
1½ cups white flour	½ cup gluten flour*
1½ cups cold water	½ teaspoon baking soda
½ cup maple-honey syrup	½ teaspoon cream of tartar
½ teaspoon ginger	2 cups oat groats*
2 tablespoons grated orange rind	4 tablespoons soft margarine
1 cup dried skim milk powder	1½ teaspoons salt
	2½ cups white flour

* See Sources of Supply.

About 7:00 in the evening stir the 1 cup starter and 1½ cups white flour together in mixing bowl (do not use metal or plastic) until it forms a ball. Let stand uncovered for 2 hours. Stir the 1½ cups cold water, ½ cup maple-honey syrup and ½ teaspoon ginger together and pour over the starter ball. Cover bowl tightly (clinging transparent wrap is good) and set in warm place (about 80°F.) overnight.

In the morning the ball of starter will have become foamy and risen to the top of the water. Beat thoroughly. Add 2 tablespoons grated orange rind, 1 cup dried skim milk and 1 cup white flour, ½ cup gluten flour, ½ teaspoon each baking soda and cream of tartar sifted together. Beat thoroughly. Add 2 cups oat groats, 4 tablespoons soft margarine and 1½ teaspoons salt. Beat well. Add 1½ cups white flour and stir until the dough clears the bowl. Spread remaining 1 cup white flour on pastry board. Turn out dough. Knead thoroughly using a little more flour if necessary to make a smooth, nonsticky dough. Cover with cloth and let rest for about 20 minutes. Divide and shape as desired. Place in greased or Teflon-coated pans. Brush tops with butter or margarine. Cover and set in warm place to rise. This bread is slow to rise so give it plenty of time. Bake in oven preheated to 350 degrees for 45 minutes for small loaves and 25 minutes for muffin rolls. If using Teflon-coated pans turn heat down to 325 during last half of baking period unless a very dark crust is desired. This recipe makes 4 high, well-rounded small loaves.

This bread is so perfect in every way—aroma, taste, texture, crust and toasting quality—that there is no need to dress it up for any occasion. The first time it was baked it was served with the following menu which remains a favorite combination for both family and company meals.

Whipped Potatoes   Creamed Salmon
Glazed Whole Red Apple Carrots*
Mixed Salad of Buttercrunch and
Ruby Lettuce, Celtuce, Curly Cress and
Chop Suey Sprigs* with Sour Cream Dressing
Oat Groats Muffin Rolls   Butter
Mulberry Jam
Russian Brown Betty (p. 168) with Ice Cream
Coffee

Soy Bread

1 cup starter
1½ cups white flour
2 cups cold water
1 teaspoon liquid artificial
    sweetener
½ teaspoon ginger
1 cup white flour
½ cup gluten flour*
½ teaspoon baking soda

½ teaspoon cream of tartar
1½ teaspoons salt
1 cup dried skim milk
    powder
1½ cups sifted soy flour*
1 cup commercial
    sour cream
4 cups white flour

About 7:00 in the evening stir the 1 cup starter and 1½ cups white flour together in mixing bowl (do not use plastic or metal) until it forms a ball. Let stand uncovered for 2 hours. Stir the 1 teaspoon liquid sweetener and ½ teaspoon ginger into the 2 cups cold water and pour over the starter ball. Cover bowl tightly (clinging transparent wrap is good) and set in warm place (about 80°F.) overnight.

In the morning the ball of starter will have become foamy and risen to the top of the water. Beat thoroughly. Add the 1 cup white flour, ½ cup gluten flour, ½ teaspoon baking soda,

* See Sources of Supply.

½ teaspoon cream of tartar and 1½ teaspoons salt sifted together. Beat thoroughly. Add the 1 cup dried skim milk and 1½ cups sifted soy flour. (This packs tightly in container and sometimes is quite lumpy. If these lumps are not broken up completely there will be hard yellowish splotches throughout the finished bread.) Mix well. Add the 1 cup sour cream and 3 cups white flour. Stir until the dough clears the bowl. Spread remaining 1 cup white flour on the pastry board. Turn out dough and knead until smooth and nonsticky using a little more flour if necessary. Cover with cloth and let rest for 10 to 20 minutes while preparing the pans. This recipe will make 4 small, high, well-rounded loaves. Butter pans generously. Divide and shape bread as desired. Place in pans. Butter tops and set in warm place to rise. When very light bake in oven preheated to 350 degrees for about 45 minutes.

This high-protein bread makes a wonderful breakfast cereal when toasted in oven until quite dry and then ground or coarsely crushed in a mortar. The salt may be omitted for those whose diets do not allow it.

Instant Potato Bread

1 cup starter
1½ cups flour
½ cup sugar
½ teaspoon ginger
2 cups cold water
⅔ cup instant mashed
   potato buds
1 cup warm water
1 cup dried skim milk
   powder

3 cups flour
½ teaspoon baking soda
½ teaspoon cream of tartar
½ cup soft butter or
   margarine
1½ teaspoons salt
4 cups flour

About 7:00 in the evening stir 1 cup starter and 1½ cups flour together in mixing bowl (do not use metal or plastic) until a soft ball is formed. Let stand uncovered for 2 hours. Stir the ½ cup sugar and ½ teaspoon ginger into the 2 cups cold water and pour over the ball of starter. Sprinkle ⅔ cup instant potato buds over the top. Cover tightly (clinging transparent wrap is good) and set in warm place (about 80°F.) overnight.

In the morning the ball of starter will have become foamy and risen to the top of the water. The potato buds will be well soaked. Beat thoroughly. Add 1 cup warm water, 1 cup dried milk and 3 cups flour sifted with ½ teaspoon each of baking soda and cream of tartar. Beat again. Add ½ cup soft shortening, 1½ teaspoons salt and 3 cups flour. Stir until the dough clears the bowl. Spread the remaining 1 cup flour on the pastry board. Turn out dough and knead thoroughly using only enough flour to make a smooth nonsticky dough. Cover with light cloth and let rest for about 20 minutes. Divide and shape as desired. Place in buttered pans, brush tops with butter, cover and let set in warm place until light. Bake in oven preheated to 350 degrees for about 45 minutes for medium loaves. If desired, for an extra rich crust, brush with cream or butter again about 5 minutes before the end of the baking period. This recipe makes 4 high, well-rounded medium loaves.

Note: Instant mashed potato buds are available commercially (I use Betty Crocker brand).

This dough is excellent for all kinds of plain rolls and buns such as Parkerhouse, crescent with seed topping, hamburger and hot dog, etc. For dessert make a rich, delicious Coffee Round:

Thumb-Print Coffee Round

1 cup Instant Potato dough	4 drops maple flavoring
3 tablespoons cashew nut butter*	Butter
	White sugar
½ cup brown sugar	Cinnamon
2 tablespoons flour	

Roll the 1 cup of dough into a circle to fit in a 9-inch layer cake pan. Place in well-buttered pan and pat out evenly to fit. Let stand a few minutes while preparing filling. Combine cashew nut butter, brown sugar, flour, maple flavoring and stir until well blended. Make three circles of thumb prints as deeply as possible in the dough, spacing the prints so that a line of 3 will center each of 8 wedge-shaped pieces when the round is cut for serving. Put an equal amount of the filling in each depression. Brush the dough between generously with butter and sprinkle with white sugar and cinnamon as thickly as desired. Let rise until very light. Bake in oven preheated to 350°F. for about 30 minutes. Serve warm.

The remaining recipes in this chapter contain 1 package unflavored gelatin which adds 7 grams protein (28 calories) to each batch of bread, as I have been informed by the research department of a large nationally known producer that the food value of the gelatin is not affected by baking temperatures. I have tried various methods of combining the gelatin with other ingredients and find no difference in results. One of the most important amino acids, lysine, combines with carbohydrates to

---

* Do use cashew butter if at all possible for it is what gives this coffee round its extra special flavor, but peanut butter can be used.

improve browning of crust and the holding quality of the gela-tin improves the texture of breads containing coarse meals and cereals, keeps the thick rich crust from crumbling badly when sliced and keeps bread moist and soft longer. (I was seeking a way to add more protein to a meatless diet when I began experimenting with the gelatin. I did not think then of the added benefits it might produce.)

Unflavored gelatin can be added to any bread recipe, either sifted with the flour or dissolved in part of the liquid.

Pineapple Bran Bread

1 cup starter
1½ cups white flour
1½ cups cold water
½ cup pineapple preserves
½ teaspoon ginger
2 cups 100% Bran Cereal
1 envelope unflavored
   gelatin
1 cup warm water

¾ cup dried buttermilk
   powder
3 cups white flour
½ teaspoon baking soda
½ teaspoon cream of tartar
1½ teaspoons salt
4 tablespoons soft butter
2 cups white flour

About 7:00 in the evening stir 1 cup starter and 1½ cups white flour together in mixing bowl (do not use metal or plastic) until a soft ball is formed. Let stand uncovered for 2 hours. Stir the 1½ cups cold water, ½ cup pineapple preserves and ½ teaspoon ginger together and pour over ball of starter. Sprinkle the 2 cups Bran Cereal over the top, cover tightly (clinging transparent wrap is good) and set in warm place (about 80°F.) overnight.

In the morning the ball of starter will have become foamy and risen to the top of the water and the cereal will be well soaked. Beat thoroughly. Stir the 1 envelope unflavored gelatin into the 1 cup warm water. Add this together with ¾ cup dried buttermilk and 3 cups white flour sifted with ½ teaspoon each baking soda and cream of tartar and 1½ teaspoons salt to the starter mix in bowl. Beat thoroughly. Add 4 tablespoons soft butter and beat again. Add 1 cup white flour and stir until the mixture clears the bowl. Spread the remaining 1 cup white flour on pastry board. Turn out dough and knead well using only enough flour to make a smooth, nonsticky dough. Cover with cloth and let rest for about 20 minutes. Prepare the pans by buttering lightly. Divide dough and shape as desired. Place in buttered pans, brush tops with butter, cover and let set in warm place until light. Bake in oven preheated to 350 degrees for about 45 minutes for small loaves. This recipe makes 4 high, well-rounded small loaves.

Use a 1-loaf portion of dough for a rich coffee cake which is soft, moist and springy:

Stripe Coffee Cake

¼ portion Pineapple Bran dough	3 tablespoons white sugar
½ cup pineapple preserves	1 teaspoon white flour
2 tablespoons soft butter	½ teaspoon mace
3 tablespoons powdered sugar	Pecan nut halves

Roll dough into rectangle to fit into a 10 x 6-inch flat pan. Butter the pan well, lay in dough and fit well into corners. With fingers or back of spoon make 3 equally spaced depressions lengthwise in the dough as deep as possible without breaking through. Dribble the pineapple preserves into these depressions. Brush the dough ridges between and the edges generously with soft butter. Mix the 3 tablespoons each of powdered and white sugar, 1 teaspoon flour and ½ teaspoon mace together and sprinkle over buttered dough stripes. Space nut halves evenly along these strips pressing in lightly. Set in warm place until very light. Bake in oven preheated to 350°F. for about 30 minutes until well done and topping and nuts are nicely toasted.

Nutlike Nutless Bread

1 cup starter
1½ cups white flour
1½ cups cold water
½ cup dark corn syrup
½ teaspoon ginger
1 cup wheat pilaf
3 cups white flour
1 envelope unflavored gelatin
½ teaspoon baking soda

½ teaspoon cream of tartar
1½ teaspoons salt
½ cup lightly toasted sesame seed
1 teaspoon maple flavoring
1 teaspoon black walnut flavoring
4 tablespoons soft butter
3 cups white flour

About 7:00 in the evening stir the 1 cup starter and 1½ cups white flour together in mixing bowl (do not use metal or plastic) until it forms a ball. Let stand uncovered about 2 hours. Stir the 1½ cups cold water, ½ cup corn syrup and ½ teaspoon ginger together and pour over starter ball. Sprinkle 1 cup wheat pilaf over top of water. Cover bowl tightly (clinging transparent wrap is good) and set in warm place (about 80°F.) overnight.

In the morning the ball of starter will have become foamy and risen to the top of the water. Beat thoroughly. Add the 3 cups white flour sifted with 1 envelope unflavored gelatin, ½ teaspoon baking soda, ½ teaspoon cream of tartar and 1½ teaspoons salt. Beat thoroughly. Add ½ cup toasted sesame seed, 1 teaspoon each of maple and black walnut flavoring and 4 tablespoons soft butter. Mix well. Add two cups white flour and stir until the dough clears the bowl. Spread remaining 1 cup of flour on the pastry board. Turn out dough and knead well using only enough flour to make a smooth nonsticky dough. Cover dough with a cloth and let rest for 10 to 20 minutes while preparing pans. This recipe will make 4 small, high, well-rounded loaves. Butter pans generously. Divide dough, shape loaves and place in pans. Butter tops. Set in warm place to rise until very light. Bake in oven preheated to 350 degrees for about 45 minutes for small loaves. Glaze crust with cream or canned milk about 5 minutes before the end of the baking period.

Some have been positive that this bread must have ground nuts in it because of the rich, nutlike taste. The addition of the gelatin prevents breads of this kind from crumbling badly when sliced.

Apple Porridge Bread

1 cup starter	Grated rind of 1 lemon
1½ cups white flour	1 cup dried skim milk
2 cups cold water	powder
½ cup brown sugar	3 cups white flour
½ teaspoon ginger	½ teaspoon baking soda
2 cups Pioneer's Porridge	½ teaspoon cream of tartar
cereal	2 teaspoons salt
2 cups applesauce	4 tablespoons soft butter
1 envelope unflavored	4½ cups white flour
gelatin	

About 7:00 in the evening stir 1 cup starter and 1½ cups white flour together in mixing bowl (do not use metal or plastic) until a soft ball is formed. Let stand uncovered for 2 hours.

Stir the ½ cup brown sugar and ½ teaspoon ginger into the 2 cups cold water. Pour over the ball of starter. Sprinkle 2 cups porridge cereal over the top. Cover bowl tightly (clinging transparent wrap is good) and set in warm place (about 80°F.) overnight.

In the morning the ball of starter will have become foamy and risen to the top and the cereal will be well soaked. Heat the 1 can applesauce enough to dissolve 1 envelope gelatin, then cool to just warm. Add to starter mixture with grated rind of lemon, 1 cup dried skim milk and 3 cups flour sifted with ½ teaspoon each of baking soda and cream of tartar. Beat well. Add 2 teaspoons salt, 4 tablespoons soft butter and 3½ cups white flour. Stir until the dough clears the bowl. Spread remaining 1 cup white flour on the pastry board. Turn out dough and knead well using a little more flour if necessary (some canned applesauce is thinner than others) to make a fairly stiff nonsticky dough. Cover with light cloth and let rest for about 20 minutes. Divide and shape as desired. Place in buttered pans, brush tops with butter, cover and let set in warm place to rise. When light, bake in-oven preheated to 350 degrees for about 45 minutes. This recipe will make 4 high, rather flat-topped loaves. This bread makes most attractive slices with its creamy color flecked with yellow lemon rind and the brown grains.

For a delightful dessert bread, add ½ to ¾ cup currants to each loaf-size portion of dough as desired. Knead in until evenly distributed, shape and bake as directed. When cool dribble thin lemon flavored icing over the loaf and sprinkle with lightly toasted chopped nuts. Without icing it is a wonderful companion to any fruit sauce when slices are toasted, buttered and eaten warm.

Note: Pioneer's Porridge is a high protein cereal of cracked grains of wheat, corn, rye, oats and rice.

6

Baking with
Buttermilk Yeast

Buttermilk Dry Yeast

2 cups buttermilk
3 cups corn meal, white
   or yellow
½ teaspoon salt

1 package dry yeast
¼ cup warm water
   Sterilized corn meal
   White flour

Scald the 2 cups of buttermilk with the 3 cups of corn meal over low fire, stirring constantly until it makes a smooth mush. Add the salt and stir well. When the mush has cooled to just warm add the dry yeast dissolved in the ¼ cup warm water. Let stand in a warm place. When it rises stir it down and let rise again three times. Add enough sterilized corn meal and white flour in equal amounts to make a very stiff dough. Use a rounding tablespoonful to make each cake. Dip them in corn meal. Lay on trays on absorbent paper and dry as quickly as possible at room temperature, turning often and changing papers as needed. Do not place in oven or in hot sun. When dry, seal each cake in transparent wrapping with tape and store in moisture-proof container in refrigerator. One cake is equal to one package of dry yeast for making starters and for overnight sponges.

Buttermilk Yeast Biscuits

1 cake homemade Butter-
milk Dry Yeast, or 1 package commercial dry yeast
1 teaspoon sugar
¼ cup warm water
2 cups buttermilk
Flour

1 cup flour
1 teaspoon sugar
½ teaspoon baking soda
½ teaspoon salt
2 tablespoons soft lard
½ cup flour
Soft butter or margarine

Dissolve yeast and sugar in the warm water. Scald buttermilk and cool to just warm. Add yeast and enough flour (about 1 cup) to the buttermilk to make a thick but pourable batter. Pour into glass jar, set in warm place to rise. Stir down and store, covered, in refrigerator.

To make biscuits take 1½ cups of this starter, add 1 cup of flour sifted with 1 teaspoon sugar, ½ teaspoon baking soda, and ½ teaspoon salt. Stir and add 2 tablespoons soft lard. Stir in about ½ cup more flour to make dough stiff enough to handle easily. Turn out on pastry board, knead lightly, roll out into square not more than ¼-inch thick. Spread with soft butter or margarine. Cut into 1½-inch strips. Stack four deep and cut into 1½-inch squares. These can be baked immediately in oven preheated to 425°F. until golden brown, stored in the refrigerator for later baking or set in a warm place for 1 to 1½ hours before baking. The flavor and texture are wonderful whatever method is used. The layers partially separate, brown beautifully on the edges and are as tender and flaky as piecrust. Add 1 cup of scalded, cooled buttermilk and 1 cup of flour each time to the starter left in the jar, allow to rise, stir down and return to the refrigerator.

There is a woman who would not think of making a stuffing

or dressing without making a batch of these biscuits, separating the layers and toasting them lightly to use in place of sliced white bread. These toasted layers are just the thing to serve in place of crackers with homemade potato soup garnished with crisp-fried crumbles of bacon.

Alaskan Sourdough Starter

1 cake Buttermilk Dry Yeast
or 1 package commercial
dry yeast
1 cup warm water

2 teaspoons salt
4 tablespoons sugar
1½ cups white flour

Prepare this the day before you wish to use it. Soak yeast in the warm water, add salt, sugar and flour, and beat well. You should have a batter which will pour but is not too thin. Keep in a warm place, tightly covered in bowl large enough to allow for it to double in volume.

Save 1 cup of this starter and store in covered pint glass jar in refrigerator. Use the remaining starter batter to make Alaskan Sourdough Pancakes. The 1 cup stored starter may be used the next time you make pancakes, or to make biscuits or fruitcake (recipes follow).

Alaskan Sourdough Pancakes

Alaskan Sourdough Starter
(full recipe less 1 cup)
2 tablespoons melted butter
1 egg, well beaten

½ teaspoon baking soda dissolved in 1 tablespoon
water

To the starter batter add the butter, egg, baking soda and water. Bake on hot griddle. This will make 12 4-inch pancakes that are delightfully tender and brown beautifully.

The next time you want to make more pancakes, make up the starter as you did the first time except use the reserved 1 cup starter instead of the dry yeast. It is important to have the batter of the proper consistency the night before using so as not to have to add either flour or liquid the next morning. Be sure to pour off the 1 cup of starter each time before adding the butter, egg and soda dissolved in water and never add any leftover pancake batter to the starter. The amount of soda may be increased slightly if for any reason the batter smells too sour.

Alaskan Sourdough Fruitcake

1½ cups golden, seedless, and puffed seeded raisins, combined
1½ cups dried currants
1 cup plus 2 tablespoons Blackberry Cordial or other wine
1 cup Alaskan Sourdough Starter
6 tablespoons butter
1 cup white sugar
1 cup brown sugar
3 eggs, well beaten
2 tablespoons grated lemon rind

4 cups white flour
1 teaspoon baking soda
1 teaspoon salt
1 teaspoon cinnamon
1 teaspoon cloves
1 teaspoon allspice
½ teaspoon mace
3 cups candied fruit: green and red cherries, pineapple, orange, citron and ginger
1 cup or more chopped nuts

Soak raisins and currants in 1 cup wine overnight. Remove starter from refrigerator and set, tightly covered, in warm place overnight. It should be in at least a two-cup container as it will just about double its volume overnight. In the morning, cream butter with sugar and beat in eggs and lemon rind. Drain wine from raisins into creamed mixture. Stir in starter and 3 cups of the flour sifted with the soda, salt and spices. Sprinkle the remaining 1 cup of flour over the fruit and nuts in a large bowl. Toss and shake until well-coated. Add to batter and mix thoroughly. Turn into loaf pans which have been generously buttered. Let stand in warm place for 30 minutes. Bake in oven preheated to 300°F. with a pan of water on floor of oven and rack as near as possible in middle of oven. Bake about 2½ hours for medium-sized loaves watching carefully to see that they do not brown too quickly. Test with toothpick. Remove from oven, turn pans on sides and allow to set for a few minutes before taking from the pans. When cold drip 2 tablespoons of wine over each cake. As soon as it is absorbed, wrap tightly in cellophane freezer paper and store in refrigerator or freezer. They improve with age.

This cake has the most beautiful golden-brown crust of any fruitcake I have ever baked and it becomes deliciously mellow and rich with age. This recipe will make 3 medium-sized loaves, but I like to bake part of it in miniature loaf pans to decorate for gifts. (The pans I have are 4½ x 2½ inches. They are made by Mirro and sold in sets of six at most large department stores. See sources of supply.)

Alaskan Sourdough Biscuits

1½ cups white flour
2 teaspoons baking powder
¼ teaspoon baking soda (½ teaspoon if starter is quite sour)
½ teaspoon salt
¼ cup butter or margarine
¼ cup cold water or milk
1 cup Alaskan Sourdough Starter

Sift dry ingredients together. Blend in butter as for piecrust. Stir water or milk into starter and mix with dry ingredients. Turn dough out onto lightly floured board and knead quickly until smooth. Roll dough out about ½ inch thick. Cut with floured cutter. Place on well greased pan. Brush with melted butter. Let rise for 1 hour in warm place. Bake in oven preheated to 425°F. for about 20 minutes. Serve hot. This recipe will make 15 or 16 biscuits with a 2-inch cutter.

These biscuits are perfect for storing in the freezer. If they are intended for this purpose just brown lightly. They may also be made ahead of time and stored in the refrigerator in the baking pans covered with transparent wrap for several hours before baking. Remove and set in warm place for 1 hour before placing in hot oven.

A modern version of Dampfnudelen, an old German pudding elegant enough to grace any table, can be made with these biscuits. For each serving allow two 2-inch biscuits, prepared as above. Place about 1 inch apart in well-buttered square layer-cake pan. Butter tops and let stand in warm place 1 hour. Bake in 425 degree oven until about half done and faintly browned. Mix ½ cup canned milk, 2 tablespoons sugar and ½ teaspoon vanilla for each 4 biscuits. Pour over biscuits and continue baking until well done and nicely browned. Remove from oven, sprinkle tops with nutmeg or mace and spoon into sauce dishes. Pour a fruit or creamy custard sauce over each portion and serve warm. (I prefer the currant-raspberry Danish junket dessert which can be prepared very quickly and makes such a beautiful color contrast; others in the family like a rich caramel custard better.)

7
Breads in Main Dishes,
Savories and Desserts

There is no other member of the family of foods as versatile as bread. It can furnish something to suit every individual taste from big, thick slabs to hide a slice of meat or cheese for a hungry man's sandwich to the thinnest, crispest piece of Melba toast for the dieting lady's lunch. It is the one food which is served in some form at every meal of the day and for snacks in between. It provides the base for savory dressings chock full of celery, sage, onions, rich broth, etc., and it can be the main ingredient in a dessert such as bread pudding. These are about the only two uses that some people make of bread in cooking and that is too bad, for there is an endless number of ways to use it in delicious dishes. Some are elegant and complicated while others are as simple and inexpensive as anyone could wish.

In the pages which follow I have included a number of favorite recipes for savory main dishes and for desserts. These will be enough to prove that a family is missing a lot if it never gets bread in any other form than slices or rolls.

Chestnut Dressing Supreme

24 dried or fresh chestnuts
2 cups rich broth
½ teaspoon curry powder
½ teaspoon mace
1 teaspoon monosodium glutamate
½ cup cream or canned milk
1 teaspoon baking powder
2 eggs
4 cups white bread crumbs
4 cups hickory-smoked corn bread crumbs

1 cup chopped celery
2 tablespoons chopped fresh parsley or 2 teaspoons parsley flakes
2 tablespoons toasted onion flakes or ½ cup finely chopped fresh onion
½ cup finely chopped fresh sage or 2 tablespoons crumbled dry sage

Simmer dried chestnuts in small amount of water until tender or, if using fresh ones, cook in small amount of water for about 15 minutes. Drain and remove shells and inner skin. Slice nuts very thin. If rich homemade broth, preferably from a pot roast simmered with wine and juniper berries, is not available use instant beef or chicken bouillon according to directions on container for 2 cups hot water. Add the curry powder, mace and monosodium glutamate to the broth and mix well. Put the crumbs, celery, parsley, onions, sage and sliced nuts in large mixing bowl. Pour over them the warm broth mixture. Mix well. Let stand about 10 minutes and mix again. Combine cream or canned milk, baking powder and eggs. Beat well. Add the beaten. egg mixture and stir thoroughly. Spoon into a buttered 2½-inch high, 9-inch square pan. Cover tightly with aluminum foil. Bake for 1 hour in oven preheated to 325°F. If it is to be served immediately, uncover and sprinkle top of dressing lightly with paprika. Place under broiler until lightly browned. If the dressing is to be stored in freezer (it improves with age) let it cool in pan then cut into fourths. Wrap in cellophane and seal. When it is to be used, let it thaw completely. Break apart with fork and pile lightly into casserole. Sprinkle top with a little cream or canned milk, cover and place in oven until heated through so that it is steaming and fluffy.

Note: For bread crumbs, break bread (see index for corn bread recipe) into small crumbs with fingers. Spread on flat pans and dry slightly in 275°F. oven while preparing the rest of the ingredients.

Stuffed Ham Rolls

Cut sticks of cold Chestnut Dressing Supreme about 1 inch square and as long as the width of thin pliable slices of cooked ham (about 3 or 4 inches) such as can be bought, packaged, in the lunch meat section. Wrap ham around dressing sticks. Lay on lightly-buttered or Teflon-coated cookie sheets. Put in oven at 300°F. until heated through. Just before serving place under broiler to crisp the ham slightly on the edges. For a buffet meal, place these on heated tray beside a bowl or little individual dishes of icy cold cranberry and raisin chutney.

Bread Sauce

2 cups rich chicken broth	1 cup bread crumbs
3 slices Canadian bacon	1 tablespoon butter
1 teaspoon toasted onion flakes	1 teaspoon lemon juice
	Minced parsley or chives

Heat broth (it should not be too highly seasoned), add the Canadian bacon cut into tiny cubes and the onion flakes. Simmer slowly for 15 minutes. Sauté the bread crumbs in the butter just until they start to brown. Add to the hot broth with 1 teaspoon lemon juice. Stir in fresh minced parsley or chives, or both, if desired. Serve at once over baked chicken breasts (rolled in any favorite coating mixture and made very crisp by placing under broiler for the last few minutes of cooking) or thick slices of other roast meats. If the broth is rich enough, any unused sauce will jell when chilled and can be cut into cubes to be served on a platter with a variety of cold cuts.

Bread Crumb Balls

3 tablespoons very fine bread crumbs
1 tablespoon deviled ham or chicken
1 teaspoon lemon rind
Salt and pepper

1 teaspoon each finely chopped fresh parsley and chives
1 teaspoon dried onion flakes
1 egg white

Mix all the ingredients together except the egg white. Stir it lightly with a fork but do not beat. Add a small amount at a time to bread crumb mixture until enough is used to bind all together. Form into tiny balls and chill. When needed, drop into hot broth or any other thin soup desired, and cook until balls rise to surface. Serve at once.

Indiana Skillet Dinner

4 large boiled potatoes
2 cups small cubes of white bread
2 tablespoons butter
Salt

Coarse black pepper
Celery salt
Paprika
2 large eggs
¼ cup cream

Cut freshly boiled potatoes into small cubes. Place with bread cubes in large heavy skillet in which the 2 tablespoons butter have been melted. Sprinkle lightly with salt, pepper, celery salt, and paprika (rotisserie seasoning may be used) and brown cubes until crisp and toasty, turning over as often as necessary. Beat 2 large eggs with ¼ cup cream (canned milk may be used) and pour over all. As soon as egg mixture has set enough fold over like an omelet. Slip onto heat-proof platter and set in oven for just a few minutes, until ready to serve. Bring to the table hot and crusty.

This dish was a childhood favorite. With a bowl of fresh-from-the-garden radishes and onions, wilted lettuce, *schmier kase* (Dutch for homemade cottage cheese from naturally soured raw milk) sprinkled with freshly grated nutmeg and a rosy red rhubarb and mulberry pie to finish the meal, what child, or grown-up either, could ask for more?

Hamburger Bun Filling

1½ pounds hamburger
¾ cups rye bread crumbs
½ cup finely chopped onion
½ cup finely chopped celery
1 cup tomato juice
½ cup catsup
3 tablespoons wine vinegar
2 tablespoons sugar
1 teaspoon monosodium glutamate
½ teaspoon garlic salt
Few grains Nepal pepper
Chopped parsley and chives

Brown hamburger in Teflon-coated or lightly-buttered skillet, breaking it apart into small crumbles as it cooks. As soon as lightly browned add rye bread crumbs, chopped onion and celery and simmer until onion and celery are clear. Add all other ingredients except parsley and chives and continue cooking over very low heat for about 30 minutes, watching carefully. Check for seasoning. Add more salt, pepper or other seasoning to suit taste. The filling should now be thick enough so that it will not drip from buns. If it is not (moisture content of hamburger varies) add a few more bread crumbs and cook a little longer until bread absorbs excess moisture. Stir in as much finely chopped parsley and chives as desired. Serve hot on big toasted buns.

I always make up twice the recipe, spoon the amount not needed for serving at once into pint containers and store in freezer. One pint will make enough filling for 4 large buns or 6 small ones.

Peppery Beef Round

4 pounds sliced, boneless beef
1 tablespoon whole black pepper
1 teaspoon whole allspice
1 teaspoon garlic salt
1 cup fine bread crumbs
1 teaspoon monosodium glutamate
1 bag herb tea
1 cup boiling water

Arrange slices of good beef, about ½ to ¾ inch thick, in a rectangle with edges overlapping so that it can be pounded into a single sheet. Crush the whole black pepper and whole allspice. Add with garlic salt and monosodium glutamate to bread crumbs (those made from a whole-grain bread are to be preferred). Mix well, sprinkle on meat and pat down to make it stay in place. Let stand while preparing 1 cup strong tea (one containing rose hips is best, do not use mint tea) by steeping 1 bag in 1 cup boiling water for 5 minutes. Roll meat very carefully so that the width of the rectangle is the length of the roll. Try not to break any of the splices open. Tie securely with heavy white cord. Place on perforated disc in heavy Dutch oven. Add the 1 cup of tea. Cover and simmer over very low heat for about 4 hours. Turn over carefully three or four times. When done, stand on end in deep bowl or stone jar, cover with broth and chill overnight before slicing. This is best served at room temperature.

Note: I prefer to use slices from a large "heel of round" roast. Lean brisket can be used.

Kansas Eggplant Casserole

½ pound hamburger
Rotisserie seasoning*
Paprika
Monosodium glutamate
1 large or 2 medium-sized eggplants
1 pint canned tomatoes or 4 large fresh tomatoes
2 to 3 cups toasted bread crumbs

2 tablespoons onion flakes or ½ cup fresh onion, finely chopped
2 tablespoons red and green chopped peppers
½ cup grated cheddar cheese or ½ can cheese soup

Sprinkle hamburger with rotisserie seasoning, paprika and monosodium glutamate. Brown well in skillet, crumbling it into bits as it cooks. In a 2-quart buttered casserole arrange layers of eggplant slices, tomatoes, hamburger and bread crumbs (if using fresh tomatoes, 2 cups crumbs will be enough to absorb juice), sprinkling each layer very lightly with rotisserie seasoning, paprika, monosodium glutamate, the chopped onions, and red and green peppers. Reserve enough bread crumbs to sprinkle on top and dribble the fat from the hamburger over these. Cover with lid or aluminum foil and bake in oven pre-

* See p. 104.

heated to 300°F. for 2½ hours. Remove cover, top with grated
cheese or soup. Sprinkle lightly with paprika. Turn heat up or
place under broiler until the cheese topping is golden and bub-
bling. This is a wonderful dish for taking to club or church
dinners as it can be prepared early in the morning. It does not
need to be piping hot to be at its best and it is even more flavorful and satisfying when reheated.

Russian Brown Betty

4 large tart apples	2 tablespoons butter
½ cup water	½ cup sugar
½ cup sugar	½ teaspoon cloves
½ to 1 cup golden raisins	Fine dry bread crumbs or
1 teaspoon grated orange	coconut meal
rind	1 teaspoon cinnamon
3 cups finely crumbled fresh	4 tablespoons strawberry
rye bread	or other preserves

Peel and core apples (Winesap or Jonathan preferred). Cut
into eighths and simmer in covered saucepan with the water, ½
cup sugar and the raisins until tender. Stir in the orange rind.
Sauté rye bread crumbs in butter just until they start to brown.
Stir in the second ½ cup sugar and the cloves. Butter a medium-
size glass loaf pan or casserole. Dust bottom and sides with fine
bread crumbs or coconut meal. Put in ⅓ of the sautéed bread
crumbs and pat into an even layer. Spoon the apples and raisins
over this layer. Sprinkle top of fruit with cinnamon. Add a
second layer of crumbs and spread the preserves over this. Top
with the remaining crumbs. Cover pan with sheet of aluminum
foil and bake in oven preheated to 325°F. for 1 hour. Remove
foil and turn heat up for just a few minutes until top is crisp

and crunchy. Serve warm or cold with ice cream or whipped topping.

The Danish version of this dessert, called Peasant Girl With Veil, omits the spices and preserves, then tops it with a layer of grated chocolate. I much prefer the Russian way but others enjoy the chocolate topping when it is served with ice cream.

Dutch Crumb Cookies

1¼ cups ground graham bread crumbs
1½ cups white flour
1 teaspoon baking soda
½ teaspoon salt
½ teaspoon nutmeg
½ cup margarine
1 cup white sugar

1 egg, well-beaten
2 teaspoons rum flavoring
1 teaspoon dehydrated lemon peel
¾ cup finely chopped English walnuts
1 cup puffed, seeded raisins
4 tablespoons boiling water

First, prepare the crumbs by drying and lightly toasting slices of graham bread before putting through food chopper or, if one is not available, put in plastic sack and crush thoroughly with rolling pin. Sift the white flour with the soda, salt and nutmeg. Cream the margarine and sugar together. Add well-beaten egg and blend thoroughly. Stir in rum flavoring and lemon peel. Add sifted flour mix, bread crumbs, chopped nuts and raisins. Stir until well mixed. Sprinkle boiling water over all and mix again. Drop from teaspoon onto lightly greased cookie sheets and bake about 15 minutes in oven preheated to 400°F. This will make 3 dozen large, crisp, crunchy cookies. They will stay crisp and crunchy, too, down to the last one if the bread crumbs are perfectly dry. They will not be nearly as nice if any moisture remains in the slices when ground.

In my opinion this is the best drop cookie recipe I have ever used. There is just one warning about making these. The dough is crunchy, too, and, if there are any boys of any size around the kitchen at baking time, quantities of it may disappear without ever getting to the oven.

New Hampshire Delight Pudding

2 heaping cups dry bread crumbs	⅔ cup white flour
¼ cup soft butter	½ teaspoon each of cloves, cinnamon, nutmeg and salt
1 egg, well beaten	2 teaspoons baking soda
½ cup molasses	⅔ cup white flour
1 cup milk	1 cup raisins or currants

Crumble bread crumbs as fine as possible with fingers (do not grind as the texture of the finished pudding will not be as light). Toss with the butter until well mixed. Add well-beaten egg, molasses and milk. Stir thoroughly. Sift the white flour with the cloves, cinnamon, nutmeg, salt and soda. Sprinkle over other ingredients in bowl. Before mixing add the raisins or currants and roll about with spoon until coated with the flour mixture. Now mix well, spoon into well-greased pudding molds, cover and steam for 2 hours on rack in covered kettle with water about halfway up on molds. Serve slightly warm with sweetened whipped cream, hard sauce or ice cream.

Crumbs from one of the brown breads such as graham or honey bran give a much richer flavor and color to this pudding.

Pear Charlotte

6 large fresh pears	4 tablespoons melted butter
½ cup sugar	½ cup sugar
2 tablespoons lemon juice	1 tablespoon grated orange
½ teaspoon mace	or lemon rind
3 cups fresh bread crumbs	

Peel, core and chop the pears. Sprinkle over them the ½ cup sugar, lemon juice and ½ teaspoon mace. Mix well. Sauté the crumbled fresh bread in butter until just beginning to brown. Stir in the second ½ cup sugar and rind. Spread ⅓ bread-crumb mixture in bottom of well-buttered medium-size glass loaf pan. Cover with ½ the fruit. Add another ⅓ of the crumbs, then the rest of the fruit and top with remaining crumbs. Sprinkle with mace. Cover with sheet of aluminum foil. Bake in oven preheated to 350°F. for about 40 minutes. Remove foil and crisp top of pudding slightly by turning up heat for a few minutes or placing under broiler. Serve warm or cold with whipped cream and Lemon Cheese (see page 77) or old-fashioned plain custard sauce.

Grandmother's English Flummery

9 small slices fresh bread	1 cup sugar
1 quart fresh berries	2 tablespoons lemon juice

Place the 9 slices of bread (Milk Pastry or Lemon Angel bread is perfect for this) in 3 layers in glass loaf pan with the crushed berries (strawberries, raspberries, blackberries or blueberries) mixed with the sugar and lemon juice spread between layers and on top. Let stand in refrigerator overnight.

This used to be placed, with the top covered with parchment paper, in the trough in the cave where spring water flowed through, keeping milk, cream and homemade butter fresh and sweet. Since it would now be inconvenient to provide the traditional English topping of clotted cream for this dish, whipped and chilled cream cheese makes a worthy substitute.

Noble Soufflé

4 slices fine white bread	¼ teaspoon salt
½ cup cream or canned milk	1 tablespoon grated lemon
2 large eggs	rind
1 cup ground or grated	1 13½-ounce can pineapple
filberts	tidbits
5 tablespoons sugar	Cinnamon

Crumble the slices of fresh soft bread. Pour the cream or canned milk over bread. When soaked, beat with a whisk until smooth. Separate the eggs. Add the well-beaten egg yolks and finely ground or grated filberts to the bread mixture. Whip the egg whites with the salt until stiff. Add the sugar, one tablespoon at a time and continue beating until very stiff. Fold gently into the bread mixture with the grated lemon rind. Place a layer of drained pineapple on bottom of a medium-size, well-buttered glass loaf pan. Sprinkle with cinnamon. Spread bread mixture over top and sprinkle it with cinnamon. Bake in oven preheated to 400°F. for about 40 minutes until firm and well browned. Serve slightly warm with ice cream or whipped topping. This makes 8 servings and is a perfect ending for a light meal of soup, crackers and relishes.

Winter Pudding

2 cups dry bread crumbs	½ teaspoon ginger
2 cups buttermilk	½ teaspoon cloves
½ cup soft butter	1 teaspoon cinnamon
2 cups brown sugar	1 teaspoon baking powder
4 tablespoons sorghum	1 teaspoon baking soda
1 cup white flour	1½ cups raisins or chopped
1 teaspoon salt	dates or very soft chopped
½ teaspoon allspice	dried apples

Stir crumbs into buttermilk (¾ cup dried powdered buttermilk may be used with 2 cups water, if fresh buttermilk is not available) and let stand for at least 30 minutes until crumbs are well soaked. Cream butter with brown sugar and sorghum. Sift all dry ingredients together. Add to creamed mixture. Add the fruit and coat with the flour mixture before beating all together. Stir in the buttermilk and crumbs. Blend well. Bake in 2 well-buttered, medium-size glass loaf pans for about 45 minutes in oven preheated to 350°F., or in 13 x 9-inch glass sheet cake pan for about 35 minutes. Serve warm or cold with whipped topping.

A long time ago this would have been served with homemade ice cream and blue damson plum preserves for a topping. The sheet cake can be very nicely cut into squares for serving, wrapped individually and frozen.

Stuffed Apples

8 large apples	4 tablespoons soft butter
1 cup currants	Apple pulp
⅔ cup sugar	¼ cup water
1 teaspoon grated lemon rind	¼ cup wine or orange juice
3 cups soft bread crumbs	Sugar
	Cinnamon

Prepare the apples by washing, coring (be careful not to cut through blossom end) and peeling just the tops. Scoop out the centers with the most effective sharp tool available such as a small serrated-tip grapefruit spoon, sharp-pointed flexible paring knife or melon ball scoop. Leave a thick enough shell to contain the stuffing. Mix the currants, sugar, lemon rind, bread crumbs (plain white bread will do but crumbs of any one of the whole-grain breads are much better) and chopped apple pulp. Fill centers of apples with this stuffing. Arrange in glass baking pan with ¼ cup water and ¼ cup wine or orange juice. Cover and bake until apples are tender and clear which should take about 1 hour at 325°F. When removed from oven and uncovered, sprinkle tops of apples with sugar and cinnamon and place pan under broiler for just a short time until topping forms a glaze. Delicious warm or cold.

Pudding in Haste

½ cup suet
4 slices soft bread
1 cup soft currants (from a freshly opened box)
4 egg yolks, well beaten
2 egg whites, stiffly beaten

1 tablespoon grated orange or lemon rind
1 teaspoon ginger or 2 tablespoons finely chopped candied ginger

Grind the suet and the bread. Add the currants and the egg yolks. Fold in the egg whites, grated rind and ginger. Mix thoroughly but gently. Shape into balls about the size of an egg. Drop into large pan of boiling water. They should be done in about 20 minutes and will rise to the top. Lift with slotted spoon. Drain on paper towels. Serve hot with rum-flavored hard sauce.

These taste very much like the old-time suet puddings which

were made every year at butchering time. They were shaped into small loaves, sewed into muslin sacks and boiled for 2 hours at least, depending on size. Then they were stored in a cold place until needed when they were heated in oven, sack removed, sliced and served with syrup or preserves.

Company Pancakes

1½ cups soft bread crumbs	½ teaspoon baking soda
2 cups buttermilk	1 tablespoon sugar
1 cup white flour	2 large eggs
1 teaspoon salt	3 tablespoons melted butter
2 teaspoons baking powder	

Soak bread crumbs in 1 cup of buttermilk (if fresh buttermilk is not available, ¾ cup dried powdered buttermilk may be used with 2 cups water). Sift together the flour, salt, baking powder, soda and sugar. Separate the eggs. Beat yolks and stir into remaining 1 cup of buttermilk. Pour into bread crumb mix. Add dry ingredients. Stir all together but do not beat. Stir in melted butter. Whip egg whites stiff and fold in gently. Bake on hot griddle at once. Will make about 16 medium cakes. For a "come-as-you-are" club breakfast serve with Medley Fruit Syrup and sour cream. It is nice to bake this batter in a Swedish Plett pan.* Keep stack of little cakes warm in oven. Serve with chilled, sweetened fresh strawberries or other fruit between cakes and top with a dollop of whipped cream and a whole fruit for a luncheon dessert.

Medley Fruit Syrup

Combine cans of three different fruits such as apple, pear and apricot, with fruit chopped fine. Add 1½ cups sugar if using

---
* See Sources of Supply.

No. 303 cans or 3 cups if using No. 2½ size cans. Add ¼ to ½ cup fresh lemon juice. Simmer until the thickness of waffle syrup. Serve cold or warm as desired.

Marguerites

Bake any favorite plain bread in No. 303 tin fruit cans. Cut into about ½-inch slices. Lightly toast on one side under broiler. Make a meringue of

2 egg whites	½ teaspoon vanilla, almond
Dash of salt	or maple flavoring
½ teaspoon cream of tartar	4 tablespoons brown sugar

Beat egg whites with salt and cream of tartar until stiff. Add flavoring and beat in brown sugar 1 tablespoon at a time. Continue beating until meringue is very stiff. Pile on untoasted sides of bread slices. This is enough for 8 or more slices depending upon how high it is desired to be. Sprinkle lightly with white sugar and cinnamon or finely chopped nuts if desired. Bake in oven preheated to 350 degrees until meringue is baked through and lightly browned. These are delightful for an after school snack with an apple or served with fresh fruit for any meal. They are best when still slightly warm or reheated for a few minutes.

Orange Crumb Cookies

2½ cups fine, dry bread crumbs	2 eggs
⅔ cup white flour	⅔ cup white sugar
1 teaspoon baking powder	2 tablespoons grated orange rind
½ teaspoon baking soda	2 tablespoons orange juice
½ teaspoon salt	¼ cup melted margarine

Toast 2½ cups fine white bread crumbs until just turning golden. Sift flour with baking powder, baking soda and salt. Beat the eggs until very light and frothy. Add sugar a little at a time and continue beating until sugar is dissolved. Add grated orange rind and orange juice with melted margarine. Stir in flour mixture and the bread crumbs. If the dough seems a little thin, let stand a few minutes until crumbs absorb excess moisture. Drop by small teaspoonfuls (for about 2½-inch cookies) on lightly greased or Teflon-coated sheets. Bake in oven preheated to 400°F. for about 10 minutes. This will make about 2½ dozen cookies. To make even more delicious sprinkle tops with white sugar and just a dash of mace or nutmeg before baking.

Candy Crumb Ice Cream Topping

1 cup dry bread crumbs
2 tablespoons butter
½ cup (or more) chopped black walnuts

½ cup brown sugar
½ teaspoon vanilla or almond flavoring

Toast bread crumbs very lightly (those made from a rich milk or egg bread are best). Melt butter in heavy skillet. Add the crumbs and stir until well mixed. Add the finely chopped nuts, brown sugar and flavoring. Cook over low heat, stirring constantly until sugar melts enough to begin to bind all together. Turn out onto very lightly buttered or Teflon-coated flat pan. When cool, break apart into fairly small crumbles. Sprinkle over ice cream just before serving. This will make enough for about 12 dishes.

It can also be stirred into about 1 quart homemade ice cream just before spooning into container for storing in freezer. It

makes a fine topping for a plain 9-inch round of dough about
½ inch thick. Sprinkle the crumbs over the buttered surface.
When round is very light, dot top all over with drops of cream
or canned milk and sprinkle with cinnamon if desired. Bake in
oven at 325°F. for about 25 minutes. It is delicious sprinkled
over plain cup custards or chilled coffee soufflé made with plain
gelatin.

Unusual Ingredients and Sources of Supply

The numbers in parentheses refer to Sources of Supply which follow the list of ingredients.

Unusual Ingredients

Banana flakes, dried (2)
Cardamom, whole (6)
Carob powder (10)
Cashew nut butter (10)
Coconut meal (2), (5), (9)
Corn meal, hickory smoked
   stone-ground (3), (9)
Corn meal, toasted (5)
Flour, graham,
   stone-ground (9)
Flour, gluten (5)
Flour, millet (8)
Flour, natural, unbleached,
   stone-ground white (9)

Flour, oat (5)
Flour, soy (5), (9)
Gossip tea (1)
Hops (6)
Maple syrup cheese (4)
Oat groats (9)
Pans, Bundt (6), (7)
Pans, Mirro (6)
Pans, Plett (6), (7)
Raw sugar (2)
Rice polish (2)
Waldmeister essence (1),
   (6)

Sources of Supply

1. Bremen House
   218 East 86th Street
   New York, New York 10028

   (Catalog) Long fluted baking tins, flavoring essences, herb teas

2. Brownville Mills
   Brownville, Nebraska 68321

   (Price list) Rice polish, rolled wheat, coconut meal, banana flakes

3. Burger's Smokehouse
   California, Missouri 65018

   Hickory smoked corn meal

4. Cheese of All Nations
   153 Chambers Street
   New York, New York 10007

   (Catalog) Maple sugar cheese, Gorgonzola with brandy spread

5. The Great Valley Mills
   Quakertown
   Buck's County, Pennsylvania 18951

   (Price list) Toasted corn meal, dark rye and many other flours and meals

6. Lekvar-By-The-Barrel
   1577 First Avenue
   New York, New York 10028

   (Catalog) Dried chestnuts, dry hops, wheat pilaf, Waldmeister and other essences, baking utensils of all kinds

7. Maid of Scandinavia
   3245 Raleigh Avenue
   Minneapolis, Minnesota 55416

   (Catalog) Candied ginger, crystal sugar, glucose, Bundt and Plett pans, many baking utensils

8. Sturd-Dee Health Products
   222 Livingston Street
   Brooklyn, New York 11201

   (Catalog) Millet, vegetable and nut oils

9. The Vermont Country Store
   Weston, Vermont 05161

   (Catalog) Stone-ground flours and meals

10. Whole Foods in Soho
    117 Prince Street
    New York, New York 10012

    (Price list) Cashew butter, carob powder

Bibliography

BACHMANN, WALTER. *Swiss Bakery and Confectionery.* London: Maclaren & Sons, Ltd., 1949.

BANFIELD, WALTER F. *Show Bread.* London: Wyman and Sons, Ltd., 1950.

BOYD, JOHN. *Morning and Hot Plate Goods.* London: Maclaren & Sons, Ltd., 1925.

COBBETT, WILLIAM. *Cottage Economy.* (17th ed.) London: Anne Cobbett, 1850.

CURTIS, ISABEL G. *Mrs. Curtis's Cook Book.* New York: Success Co., 1909.

GRIBBEN, H. *Vienna and Other Fancy Breads.* London: Maclaren & Sons, Ltd., 1900.

HANDY, AMY L. *Wartime Breads and Cakes.* Boston: Houghton Mifflin Co., 1918.

HEATH, AMBROSE. *Good Cooking with Yeast.* London: Faber and Faber, 1940.

HOUNIHAN, JOHN D. *Bakers and Confectioners, Guide and Treasure.* Staunton, Va.: John D. Hounihan, 1877.

RORER, MRS. S. T. *Bread and Bread Making.* Philadelphia: George Buchanan & Co., 1900.

SHEPPARD, RONALD AND NEWTON, EDWARD. *The Story of Bread.* London: Routledge & Regan Paul, 1957.

SIMMONS, OWEN. *The Book of Bread*. London: Maclaren & Sons, Ltd., 1900.

SPICER, DOROTHY G. *From an English Oven*. New York: The Women's Press, 1948.

STORCK, JOHN AND TEAGUE, WALTER D. *Flour For Man's Bread*. Minneapolis: Minnesota Press, 1952.

SUMPTION, LOIS L. AND ASHBROOK, MARGUERITE L. *Breads and More Breads*. Peoria, Ill.: Manual Arts Press, 1941.

WELLS, ROBERT. *The New System of Making Breads*. London: Heywood & Son, 1903.

WIHLFAHRT, JULIUS E. *Treatise on Baking*. London: C. Souer & Co., 1907.

Domestic Cookery, Enquire Within Upon Everything and The White House Cook Book have also been used for reference but as their bindings and front pages are missing, I can give no information as to author, publisher, and edition.

Index

A CATALOGUE OF
SELECTED DOVER BOOKS
IN ALL FIELDS OF INTEREST

A CATALOGUE OF SELECTED DOVER BOOKS IN ALL FIELDS OF INTEREST

CELESTIAL OBJECTS FOR COMMON TELESCOPES, T. W. Webb. The most used book in amateur astronomy: inestimable aid for locating and identifying nearly 4,000 celestial objects. Edited, updated by Margaret W. Mayall. 77 illustrations. Total of 645pp. 5⅜ x 8½.
20917-2, 20918-0 Pa., Two-vol. set **$10.00**

HISTORICAL STUDIES IN THE LANGUAGE OF CHEMISTRY, M. P. Crosland. The important part language has played in the development of chemistry from the symbolism of alchemy to the adoption of systematic nomenclature in 1892. ". . . wholeheartedly recommended,"—Science. 15 illustrations. 416pp. of text. 5⅝ x 8¼. 63702-6 Pa. **$7.50**

BURNHAM'S CELESTIAL HANDBOOK, Robert Burnham, Jr. Thorough, readable guide to the stars beyond our solar system. Exhaustive treatment, fully illustrated. Breakdown is alphabetical by constellation: Andromeda to Cetus in Vol. 1; Chamaeleon to Orion in Vol. 2; and Pavo to Vulpecula in Vol. 3. Hundreds of illustrations. Total of about 2000pp. 6⅛ x 9¼.
23567-X, 23568-8, 23673-0 Pa., Three-vol. set **$32.85**

THEORY OF WING SECTIONS: INCLUDING A SUMMARY OF AIR-FOIL DATA, Ira H. Abbott and A. E. von Doenhoff. Concise compilation of subatomic aerodynamic characteristics of modern NASA wing sections, plus description of theory. 350pp. of tables. 693pp. 5⅜ x 8½.
60586-8 Pa. **$9.95**

DE RE METALLICA, Georgius Agricola. Translated by Herbert C. Hoover and Lou H. Hoover. The famous Hoover translation of greatest treatise on technological chemistry, engineering, geology, mining of early modern times (1556). All 289 original woodcuts. 638pp. 6¾ x 11.
60006-8 Clothbd. **$19.95**

THE ORIGIN OF CONTINENTS AND OCEANS, Alfred Wegener. One of the most influential, most controversial books in science, the classic statement for continental drift. Full 1966 translation of Wegener's final (1929) version. 64 illustrations. 246pp. 5⅜ x 8½.(EBE)61708-4 Pa. **$5.00**

THE PRINCIPLES OF PSYCHOLOGY, William James. Famous long course complete, unabridged. Stream of thought, time perception, memory, experimental methods; great work decades ahead of its time. Still valid, useful; read in many classes. 94 figures. Total of 1391pp. 5⅜ x 8½.
20381-6, 20382-4 Pa., Two-vol. set **$19.90**

CATALOGUE OF DOVER BOOKS

YUCATAN BEFORE AND AFTER THE CONQUEST, Diego de Landa. First English translation of basic book in Maya studies, the only significant account of Yucatan written in the early post-Conquest era. Translated by distinguished Maya scholar William Gates. Appendices, introduction, 4 maps and over 120 illustrations added by translator. 162pp. 5⅜ x 8½.
23622-6 Pa. $3.50

THE MALAY ARCHIPELAGO, Alfred R. Wallace. Spirited travel account by one of founders of modern biology. Touches on zoology, botany, ethnography, geography, and geology. 62 illustrations, maps. 515pp. 5⅜ x 8½.
20187-2 Pa. $6.95

THE DISCOVERY OF THE TOMB OF TUTANKHAMEN, Howard Carter, A. C. Mace. Accompany Carter in the thrill of discovery, as ruined passage suddenly reveals unique, untouched, fabulously rich tomb. Fascinating account, with 106 illustrations. New introduction by J. M. White. Total of 382pp. 5⅜ x 8½. (Available in U.S. only) 23500-9 Pa. $5.50

THE WORLD'S GREATEST SPEECHES, edited by Lewis Copeland and Lawrence W. Lamm. Vast collection of 278 speeches from Greeks up to present. Powerful and effective models; unique look at history. Revised to 1970. Indices. 842pp. 5⅜ x 8½. 20468-5 Pa. $9.95

THE 100 GREATEST ADVERTISEMENTS, Julian Watkins. The priceless ingredient; His master's voice; 99 44/100% pure; over 100 others. How they were written, their impact, etc. Remarkable record. 130 illustrations. 233pp. 7⅞ x 10 3/5. 20540-1 Pa. $6.95

CRUICKSHANK PRINTS FOR HAND COLORING, George Cruickshank. 18 illustrations, one side of a page, on fine-quality paper suitable for watercolors. Caricatures of people in society (c. 1820) full of trenchant wit. Very large format. 32pp. 11 x 16. 23684-6 Pa. $6.00

THIRTY-TWO COLOR POSTCARDS OF TWENTIETH-CENTURY AMERICAN ART, Whitney Museum of American Art. Reproduced in full color in postcard form are 31 art works and one shot of the museum. Calder, Hopper, Rauschenberg, others. Detachable. 16pp. 8¼ x 11.
23629-3 Pa. $3.50

MUSIC OF THE SPHERES: THE MATERIAL UNIVERSE FROM ATOM TO QUASAR SIMPLY EXPLAINED, Guy Murchie. Planets, stars, geology, atoms, radiation, relativity, quantum theory, light, antimatter, similar topics. 319 figures. 664pp. 5⅜ x 8½.
21809-0, 21810-4 Pa., Two-vol. set $11.00

EINSTEIN'S THEORY OF RELATIVITY, Max Born. Finest semi-technical account; covers Einstein, Lorentz, Minkowski, and others, with much detail, much explanation of ideas and math not readily available elsewhere on this level. For student, non-specialist. 376pp. 5⅜ x 8½.
60769-0 Pa. $5.00

THE SENSE OF BEAUTY, George Santayana. Masterfully written discussion of nature of beauty, materials of beauty, form, expression; art, literature, social sciences all involved. 168pp. 5⅜ x 8½.   20238-0 Pa. $3.50

ON THE IMPROVEMENT OF THE UNDERSTANDING, Benedict Spinoza. Also contains *Ethics, Correspondence,* all in excellent R. Elwes translation. Basic works on entry to philosophy, pantheism, exchange of ideas with great contemporaries. 402pp. 5⅜ x 8½.   20250-X Pa. $5.95

THE TRAGIC SENSE OF LIFE, Miguel de Unamuno. Acknowledged masterpiece of existential literature, one of most important books of 20th century. Introduction by Madariaga. 367pp. 5⅜ x 8½.
20257-7 Pa. $6.00

THE GUIDE FOR THE PERPLEXED, Moses Maimonides. Great classic of medieval Judaism attempts to reconcile revealed religion (Pentateuch, commentaries) with Aristotelian philosophy. Important historically, still relevant in problems. Unabridged Friedlander translation. Total of 473pp. 5⅜ x 8½.   20351-4 Pa. $6.95

THE I CHING (THE BOOK OF CHANGES), translated by James Legge. Complete translation of basic text plus appendices by Confucius, and Chinese commentary of most penetrating divination manual ever prepared. Indispensable to study of early Oriental civilizations, to modern inquiring reader. 448pp. 5⅜ x 8½.   21062-6 Pa. $6.00

THE EGYPTIAN BOOK OF THE DEAD, E. A. Wallis Budge. Complete reproduction of Ani's papyrus, finest ever found. Full hieroglyphic text, interlinear transliteration, word for word translation, smooth translation. Basic work, for Egyptology, for modern study of psychic matters. Total of 533pp. 6½ x 9¼. (USCO)   21866-X Pa. $8.50

THE GODS OF THE EGYPTIANS, E. A. Wallis Budge. Never excelled for richness, fullness: all gods, goddesses, demons, mythical figures of Ancient Egypt; their legends, rites, incarnations, variations, powers, etc. Many hieroglyphic texts cited. Over 225 illustrations, plus 6 color plates. Total of 988pp. 6⅛ x 9¼. (EBE)
22055-9, 22056-7 Pa., Two-vol. set $20.00

THE STANDARD BOOK OF QUILT MAKING AND COLLECTING, Marguerite Ickis. Full information, full-sized patterns for making 46 traditional quilts, also 150 other patterns. Quilted cloths, lame, satin quilts, etc. 483 illustrations. 273pp. 6⅞ x 9⅝.   20582-7 Pa. $5.95

CORAL GARDENS AND THEIR MAGIC, Bronsilaw Malinowski. Classic study of the methods of tilling the soil and of agricultural rites in the Trobriand Islands of Melanesia. Author is one of the most important figures in the field of modern social anthropology. 143 illustrations. Indexes. Total of 911pp. of text. 5⅝ x 8¼. (Available in U.S. only)
23597-1 Pa. $12.95

CATALOGUE OF DOVER BOOKS

THE PHILOSOPHY OF HISTORY, Georg W. Hegel. Great classic of Western thought develops concept that history is not chance but a rational process, the evolution of freedom. 457pp. 5⅜ x 8½.   20112-0 Pa. $6.50

LANGUAGE, TRUTH AND LOGIC, Alfred J. Ayer. Famous, clear introduction to Vienna, Cambridge schools of Logical Positivism. Role of philosophy, elimination of metaphysics, nature of analysis, etc. 160pp. 5⅜ x 8½. (USCO)   20010-8 Pa. $2.75

A PREFACE TO LOGIC, Morris R. Cohen. Great City College teacher in renowned, easily followed exposition of formal logic, probability, values, logic and world order and similar topics; no previous background needed. 209pp. 5⅜ x 8½.   23517-3 Pa. $4.95

REASON AND NATURE, Morris R. Cohen. Brilliant analysis of reason and its multitudinous ramifications by charismatic teacher. Interdisciplinary, synthesizing work widely praised when it first appeared in 1931. Second (1953) edition. Indexes. 496pp. 5⅜ x 8½.   23633-1 Pa. $7.50

AN ESSAY CONCERNING HUMAN UNDERSTANDING, John Locke. The only complete edition of enormously important classic, with authoritative editorial material by A. C. Fraser. Total of 1176pp. 5⅜ x 8½.
20530-4, 20531-2 Pa., Two-vol. set $17.90

HANDBOOK OF MATHEMATICAL FUNCTIONS WITH FORMULAS, GRAPHS, AND MATHEMATICAL TABLES, edited by Milton Abramowitz and Irene A. Stegun. Vast compendium: 29 sets of tables, some to as high as 20 places. 1,046pp. 8 x 10½.   61272-4 Pa. $19.95

MATHEMATICS FOR THE PHYSICAL SCIENCES, Herbert S. Wilf. Highly acclaimed work offers clear presentations of vector spaces and matrices, orthogonal functions, roots of polynomial equations, conformal mapping, calculus of variations, etc. Knowledge of theory of functions of real and complex variables is assumed. Exercises and solutions. Index. 284pp. 5⅝ x 8¼.   63635-6 Pa. $5.00

THE PRINCIPLE OF RELATIVITY, Albert Einstein et al. Eleven most important original papers on special and general theories. Seven by Einstein, two by Lorentz, one each by Minkowski and Weyl. All translated, unabridged. 216pp. 5⅜ x 8½.   60081-5 Pa. $3.50

THERMODYNAMICS, Enrico Fermi. A classic of modern science. Clear, organized treatment of systems, first and second laws, entropy, thermodynamic potentials, gaseous reactions, dilute solutions, entropy constant. No math beyond calculus required. Problems. 160pp. 5⅜ x 8½.
60361-X Pa. $4.00

ELEMENTARY MECHANICS OF FLUIDS, Hunter Rouse. Classic undergraduate text widely considered to be far better than many later books. Ranges from fluid velocity and acceleration to role of compressibility in fluid motion. Numerous examples, questions, problems. 224 illustrations. 376pp. 5⅝ x 8¼.   63699-2 Pa. $7.00

THE AMERICAN SENATOR, Anthony Trollope. Little known, long unavailable Trollope novel on a grand scale. Here are humorous comment on American vs. English culture, and stunning portrayal of a heroine/villainess. Superb evocation of Victorian village life. 561pp. 5⅜ x 8½.
23801-6 Pa. $7.95

WAS IT MURDER? James Hilton. The author of *Lost Horizon* and *Goodbye, Mr. Chips* wrote one detective novel (under a pen-name) which was quickly forgotten and virtually lost, even at the height of Hilton's fame. This edition brings it back—a finely crafted public school puzzle resplendent with Hilton's stylish atmosphere. A thoroughly English thriller by the creator of Shangri-la. 252pp. 5⅜ x 8. (Available in U.S. only)
23774-5 Pa. $3.00

CENTRAL PARK: A PHOTOGRAPHIC GUIDE, Victor Laredo and Henry Hope Reed. 121 superb photographs show dramatic views of Central Park: Bethesda Fountain, Cleopatra's Needle, Sheep Meadow, the Blockhouse, plus people engaged in many park activities: ice skating, bike riding, etc. Captions by former Curator of Central Park, Henry Hope Reed, provide historical view, changes, etc. Also photos of N.Y. landmarks on park's periphery. 96pp. 8½ x 11. 23750-8 Pa. $4.95

NANTUCKET IN THE NINETEENTH CENTURY, Clay Lancaster. 180 rare photographs, stereographs, maps, drawings and floor plans recreate unique American island society. Authentic scenes of shipwreck, lighthouses, streets, homes are arranged in geographic sequence to provide walking-tour guide to old Nantucket existing today. Introduction, captions. 160pp. 8⅞ x 11¾. 23747-8 Pa. $7.95

STONE AND MAN: A PHOTOGRAPHIC EXPLORATION, Andreas Feininger. 106 photographs by *Life* photographer Feininger portray man's deep passion for stone through the ages. Stonehenge-like megaliths, fortified towns, sculpted marble and crumbling tenements show textures, beauties, fascination. 128pp. 9¼ x 10¾. 23756-7 Pa. $6.95

CIRCLES, A MATHEMATICAL VIEW, D. Pedoe. Fundamental aspects of college geometry, non-Euclidean geometry, and other branches of mathematics: representing circle by point. Poincare model, isoperimetric property, etc. Stimulating recreational reading. 66 figures. 96pp. 5⅝ x 8¼.
63698-4 Pa. $3.50

THE DISCOVERY OF NEPTUNE, Morton Grosser. Dramatic scientific history of the investigations leading up to the actual discovery of the eighth planet of our solar system. Lucid, well-researched book by well-known historian of science. 172pp. 5⅜ x 8½. 23726-5 Pa. $3.95

THE DEVIL'S DICTIONARY. Ambrose Bierce. Barbed, bitter, brilliant witticisms in the form of a dictionary. Best, most ferocious satire America has produced. 145pp. 5⅜ x 8½. 20487-1 Pa. $2.50

CATALOGUE OF DOVER BOOKS

THE ART OF THE CINEMATOGRAPHER, Leonard Maltin. Survey of American cinematography history and anecdotal interviews with 5 masters—Arthur Miller, Hal Mohr, Hal Rosson, Lucien Ballard, and Conrad Hall. Very large selection of behind-the-scenes production photos. 105 photographs. Filmographies. Index. Originally *Behind the Camera.* 144pp. 8¼ x 11. 23686-2 Pa. $5.00

THE COMPLETE NONSENSE OF EDWARD LEAR, Edward Lear. All nonsense limericks, zany alphabets, Owl and Pussycat, songs, nonsense botany, etc., illustrated by Lear. Total of 321pp. 5⅜ x 8½. (Available in U.S. only) 20167-8 Pa. $4.50

INGENIOUS MATHEMATICAL PROBLEMS AND METHODS, Louis A. Graham. Sophisticated material from Graham *Dial,* applied and pure; stresses solution methods. Logic, number theory, networks, inversions, etc. 237pp. 5⅜ x 8½. 20545-2 Pa. $4.95

BEST MATHEMATICAL PUZZLES OF SAM LOYD, edited by Martin Gardner. Bizarre, original, whimsical puzzles by America's greatest puzzler. From fabulously rare *Cyclopedia,* including famous 14-15 puzzles, the Horse of a Different Color, 115 more. Elementary math. 150 illustrations. 167pp. 5⅜ x 8½. 20498-7 Pa. $3.50

THE BASIS OF COMBINATION IN CHESS, J. du Mont. Easy-to-follow, instructive book on elements of combination play, with chapters on each piece and every powerful combination team—two knights, bishop and knight, rook and bishop, etc. 250 diagrams. 218pp. 5⅜ x 8½. (Available in U.S. only) 23644-7 Pa. $4.50

MODERN CHESS STRATEGY, Ludek Pachman. The use of the queen, the active king, exchanges, pawn play, the center, weak squares, etc. Section on rook alone worth price of the book. Stress on the moderns. Often considered the most important book on strategy. 314pp. 5⅜ x 8½. 20290-9 Pa. $5.00

LASKER'S MANUAL OF CHESS, Dr. Emanuel Lasker. Great world champion offers very thorough coverage of all aspects of chess. Combinations, position play, openings, end game, aesthetics of chess, philosophy of struggle, much more. Filled with analyzed games. 390pp. 5⅜ x 8½. 20640-8 Pa. $5.95

500 MASTER GAMES OF CHESS, S. Tartakower, J. du Mont. Vast collection of great chess games from 1798-1938, with much material nowhere else readily available. Fully annotated, arranged by opening for easier study. 664pp. 5⅜ x 8½. 23208-5 Pa. $8.50

A GUIDE TO CHESS ENDINGS, Dr. Max Euwe, David Hooper. One of the finest modern works on chess endings. Thorough analysis of the most frequently encountered endings by former world champion. 331 examples, each with diagram. 248pp. 5⅜ x 8½. 23332-4 Pa. $3.95

THE COMPLETE BOOK OF DOLL MAKING AND COLLECTING, Catherine Christopher. Instructions, patterns for dozens of dolls, from rag doll on up to elaborate, historically accurate figures. Mould faces, sew clothing, make doll houses, etc. Also collecting information. Many illustrations. 288pp. 6 x 9. 22066-4 Pa. $4.95

THE DAGUERREOTYPE IN AMERICA, Beaumont Newhall. Wonderful portraits, 1850's townscapes, landscapes; full text plus 104 photographs. The basic book. Enlarged 1976 edition. 272pp. 8¼ x 11¼.
23322-7 Pa. $7.95

CRAFTSMAN HOMES, Gustav Stickley. 296 architectural drawings, floor plans, and photographs illustrate 40 different kinds of "Mission-style" homes from *The Craftsman* (1901-16), voice of American style of simplicity and organic harmony. Thorough coverage of Craftsman idea in text and picture, now collector's item. 224pp. 8⅛ x 11. 23791-5 Pa. $6.50

PEWTER-WORKING: INSTRUCTIONS AND PROJECTS, Burl N. Osborn. & Gordon O. Wilber. Introduction to pewter-working for amateur craftsman. History and characteristics of pewter; tools, materials, step-by-step instructions. Photos, line drawings, diagrams. Total of 160pp. 7⅞ x 10¾. 23786-9 Pa. $4.50

THE GREAT CHICAGO FIRE, edited by David Lowe. 10 dramatic, eye-witness accounts of the 1871 disaster, including one of the aftermath and rebuilding, plus 70 contemporary photographs and illustrations of the ruins—courthouse, Palmer House, Great Central Depot, etc. Introduction by David Lowe. 87pp. 8¼ x 11. 23771-0 Pa. $4.95

SILHOUETTES: A PICTORIAL ARCHIVE OF VARIED ILLUSTRATIONS, edited by Carol Belanger Grafton. Over 600 silhouettes from the 18th to 20th centuries include profiles and full figures of men and women, children, birds and animals, groups and scenes, nature, ships, an alphabet. Dozens of uses for commercial artists and craftspeople. 144pp. 8⅜ x 11¼.
23781-8 Pa. $4.50

ANIMALS: 1,419 COPYRIGHT-FREE ILLUSTRATIONS OF MAMMALS, BIRDS, FISH, INSECTS, ETC., edited by Jim Harter. Clear wood engravings present, in extremely lifelike poses, over 1,000 species of animals. One of the most extensive copyright-free pictorial sourcebooks of its kind. Captions. Index. 284pp. 9 x 12. 23766-4 Pa. $8.95

INDIAN DESIGNS FROM ANCIENT ECUADOR, Frederick W. Shaffer. 282 original designs by pre-Columbian Indians of Ecuador (500-1500 A.D.). Designs include people, mammals, birds, reptiles, fish, plants, heads, geometric designs. Use as is or alter for advertising, textiles, leathercraft, etc. Introduction. 95pp. 8¾ x 11¼. 23764-8 Pa. $4.95

SZIGETI ON THE VIOLIN, Joseph Szigeti. Genial, loosely structured tour by premier violinist, featuring a pleasant mixture of reminiscenes, insights into great music and musicians, innumerable tips for practicing violinists. 385 musical passages. 256pp. 5⅝ x 8¼. 23763-X Pa. $5.00

TONE POEMS, SERIES II: TILL EULENSPIEGELS LUSTIGE STREICHE, ALSO SPRACH ZARATHUSTRA, AND EIN HELDEN-LEBEN, Richard Strauss. Three important orchestral works, including very popular *Till Eulenspiegel's Marry Pranks,* reproduced in full score from original editions. Study score. 315pp. 9⅜ x 12¼. (Available in U.S. only)
23755-9 Pa. $9.95

TONE POEMS, SERIES I: DON JUAN, TOD UND VERKLARUNG AND DON QUIXOTE, Richard Strauss. Three of the most often performed and recorded works in entire orchestral repertoire, reproduced in full score from original editions. Study score. 286pp. 9⅜ x 12¼. (Available in U.S. only)
23754-0 Pa. $9.95

11 LATE STRING QUARTETS, Franz Joseph Haydn. The form which Haydn defined and "brought to perfection." (*Grove's*). 11 string quartets in complete score, his last and his best. The first in a projected series of the complete Haydn string quartets. Reliable modern Eulenberg edition, otherwise difficult to obtain. 320pp. 8⅜ x 11¼. (Available in U.S. only)
23753-2 Pa. $8.95

FOURTH, FIFTH AND SIXTH SYMPHONIES IN FULL SCORE, Peter Ilyitch Tchaikovsky. Complete orchestral scores of Symphony No. 4 in F Minor, Op. 36; Symphony No. 5 in E Minor, Op. 64; Symphony No. 6 in B Minor, "Pathetique," Op. 74. Bretikopf & Hartel eds. Study score. 480pp. 9⅜ x 12¼. 23861-X Pa. $12.95

THE MARRIAGE OF FIGARO: COMPLETE SCORE, Wolfgang A. Mozart. Finest comic opera ever written. Full score, not to be confused with piano renderings. Peters edition. Study score. 448pp. 9⅜ x 12¼. (Available in U.S. only)
23751-6 Pa. $13.95

"IMAGE" ON THE ART AND EVOLUTION OF THE FILM, edited by Marshall Deutelbaum. Pioneering book brings together for first time 38 groundbreaking articles on early silent films from *Image* and 263 illustrations newly shot from rare prints in the collection of the International Museum of Photography. A landmark work. Index. 256pp. 8¼ x 11.
23777-X Pa. $8.95

AROUND-THE-WORLD COOKY BOOK, Lois Lintner Sumption and Marguerite Lintner Ashbrook. 373 cooky and frosting recipes from 28 countries (America, Austria, China, Russia, Italy, etc.) include Viennese kisses, rice wafers, London strips, lady fingers, hony, sugar spice, maple cookies, etc. Clear instructions. All tested. 38 drawings. 182pp. 5⅜ x 8.
23802-4 Pa. $2.75

THE ART NOUVEAU STYLE, edited by Roberta Waddell. 579 rare photographs, not available elsewhere, of works in jewelry, metalwork, glass, ceramics, textiles, architecture and furniture by 175 artists—Mucha, Seguy, Lalique, Tiffany, Gaudin, Hohlwein, Saarinen, and many others. 288pp. 8⅜ x 11¼. 23515-7 Pa. $8.95

CATALOGUE OF DOVER BOOKS

THE CURVES OF LIFE, Theodore A. Cook. Examination of shells, leaves, horns, human body, art, etc., in *"the* classic reference on how the golden ratio applies to spirals and helices in nature . . . ."—Martin Gardner. 426 illustrations. Total of 512pp. 5⅜ x 8½.   23701-X Pa. $6.95

AN ILLUSTRATED FLORA OF THE NORTHERN UNITED STATES AND CANADA, Nathaniel L. Britton, Addison Brown. Encyclopedic work covers 4666 species, ferns on up. Everything. Full botanical information, illustration for each. This earlier edition is preferred by many to more recent revisions. 1913 edition. Over 4000 illustrations, total of 2087pp. 6⅛ x 9¼.   22642-5, 22643-3, 22644-1 Pa., Three-vol. set $28.50

MANUAL OF THE GRASSES OF THE UNITED STATES, A. S. Hitchcock, U.S. Dept. of Agriculture. The basic study of American grasses, both indigenous and escapes, cultivated and wild. Over 1100 species. Full descriptions, information. Over 1100 maps, illustrations. Total of 1051pp. 5⅜ x 8½.   22717-0, 22718-9 Pa., Two-vol. set $17.00

THE CACTACEAE,, Nathaniel L. Britton, John N. Rose. Exhaustive, definitive. Every cactus in the world. Full botanical descriptions. Thorough statement of nomenclatures, habitat, detailed finding keys. The one book needed by every cactus enthusiast. Over 1275 illustrations. Total of 1080pp. 8 x 10¼.   21191-6, 21192-4 Clothbd., Two-vol. set $50.00

AMERICAN MEDICINAL PLANTS, Charles F. Millspaugh. Full descriptions, 180 plants covered: history; physical description; methods of preparation with all chemical constituents extracted; all claimed curative or adverse effects. 180 full-page plates. Classification table. 804pp. 6½ x 9¼.
23034-1 Pa. $13.95

A MODERN HERBAL, Margaret Grieve. Much the fullest, most exact, most useful compilation of herbal material. Gigantic alphabetical encyclopedia, from aconite to zedoary, gives botanical information, medical properties, folklore, economic uses, and much else. Indispensable to serious reader. 161 illustrations. 888pp. 6½ x 9¼. (Available in U.S. only)
22798-7, 22799-5 Pa., Two-vol. set $15.00

THE HERBAL or GENERAL HISTORY OF PLANTS, John Gerard. The 1633 edition revised and enlarged by Thomas Johnson. Containing almost 2850 plant descriptions and 2705 superb illustrations, Gerard's *Herbal* is a monumental work, the book all modern English herbals are derived from, the one herbal every serious enthusiast should have in its entirety. Original editions are worth perhaps $750. 1678pp. 8½ x 12¼.
23147-X Clothbd. $75.00

MANUAL OF THE TREES OF NORTH AMERICA, Charles S. Sargent. The basic survey of every native tree and tree-like shrub, 717 species in all. Extremely full descriptions, information on habitat, growth, locales, economics, etc. Necessary to every serious tree lover. Over 100 finding keys. 783 illustrations. Total of 986pp. 5⅜ x 8½.
20277-1, 20278-X Pa., Two-vol. set $12.00

CATALOGUE OF DOVER BOOKS

GREAT NEWS PHOTOS AND THE STORIES BEHIND THEM, John Faber. Dramatic volume of 140 great news photos, 1855 through 1976, and revealing stories behind them, with both historical and technical information. Hindenburg disaster, shooting of Oswald, nomination of Jimmy Carter, etc. 160pp. 8¼ x 11. 23667-6 Pa. $6.00

CRUICKSHANK'S PHOTOGRAPHS OF BIRDS OF AMERICA, Allan D. Cruickshank. Great ornithologist, photographer presents 177 closeups, groupings, panoramas, flightings, etc., of about 150 different birds. Expanded *Wings in the Wilderness*. Introduction by Helen G. Cruickshank. 191pp. 8¼ x 11. 23497-5 Pa. $7.95

AMERICAN WILDLIFE AND PLANTS, A. C. Martin, et al. Describes food habits of more than 1000 species of mammals, birds, fish. Special treatment of important food plants. Over 300 illustrations. 500pp. 5⅜ x 8½. 20793-5 Pa. $6.50

THE PEOPLE CALLED SHAKERS, Edward D. Andrews. Lifetime of research, definitive study of Shakers: origins, beliefs, practices, dances, social organization, furniture and crafts, impact on 19th-century USA, present heritage. Indispensable to student of American history, collector. 33 illustrations. 351pp. 5⅜ x 8½. 21081-2 Pa. $5.50

OLD NEW YORK IN EARLY PHOTOGRAPHS, Mary Black. New York City as it was in 1853-1901, through 196 wonderful photographs from N.-Y. Historical Society. Great Blizzard, Lincoln's funeral procession, great buildings. 228pp. 9 x 12. 22907-6 Pa. $9.95

MR. LINCOLN'S CAMERA MAN: MATHEW BRADY, Roy Meredith. Over 300 Brady photos reproduced directly from original negatives, photos. Jackson, Webster, Grant, Lee, Carnegie, Barnum; Lincoln; Battle Smoke, Death of Rebel Sniper, Atlanta Just After Capture. Lively commentary. 368pp. 8⅜ x 11¼. 23021-X Pa. $11.95

TRAVELS OF WILLIAM BARTRAM, William Bartram. From 1773-8, Bartram explored Northern Florida, Georgia, Carolinas, and reported on wild life, plants, Indians, early settlers. Basic account for period, entertaining reading. Edited by Mark Van Doren. 13 illustrations. 141pp. 5⅜ x 8½. 20013-2 Pa. $6.00

THE GENTLEMAN AND CABINET MAKER'S DIRECTOR, Thomas Chippendale. Full reprint, 1762 style book, most influential of all time; chairs, tables, sofas, mirrors, cabinets, etc. 200 plates, plus 24 photographs of surviving pieces. 249pp. 9⅞ x 12¾. 21601-2 Pa. $8.95

AMERICAN CARRIAGES, SLEIGHS, SULKIES AND CARTS, edited by Don H. Berkebile. 168 Victorian illustrations from catalogues, trade journals, fully captioned. Useful for artists. Author is Assoc. Curator, Div. of Transportation of Smithsonian Institution. 168pp. 8½ x 9½. 23328-6 Pa. $6.50

SECOND PIATIGORSKY CUP, edited by Isaac Kashdan. One of the greatest tournament books ever produced in the English language. All 90 games of the 1966 tournament, annotated by players, most annotated by both players. Features Petrosian, Spassky, Fischer, Larsen, six others. 228pp. 5⅜ x 8½. 23572-6 Pa. $3.50

ENCYCLOPEDIA OF CARD TRICKS, revised and edited by Jean Hugard. How to perform over 600 card tricks, devised by the world's greatest magicians: impromptus, spelling tricks, key cards, using special packs, much, much more. Additional chapter on card technique. 66 illustrations. 402pp. 5⅜ x 8½. (Available in U.S. only) 21252-1 Pa. $5.95

MAGIC: STAGE ILLUSIONS, SPECIAL EFFECTS AND TRICK PHOTOGRAPHY, Albert A. Hopkins, Henry R. Evans. One of the great classics; fullest, most authorative explanation of vanishing lady, levitations, scores of other great stage effects. Also small magic, automata, stunts. 446 illustrations. 556pp. 5⅜ x 8½. 23344-8 Pa. $6.95

THE SECRETS OF HOUDINI, J. C. Cannell. Classic study of Houdini's incredible magic, exposing closely-kept professional secrets and revealing, in general terms, the whole art of stage magic. 67 illustrations. 279pp. 5⅜ x 8½. 22913-0 Pa. $5.95

HOFFMANN'S MODERN MAGIC, Professor Hoffmann. One of the best, and best-known, magicians' manuals of the past century. Hundreds of tricks from card tricks and simple sleight of hand to elaborate illusions involving construction of complicated machinery. 332 illustrations. 563pp. 5⅜ x 8½. 23623-4 Pa. $6.95

THOMAS NAST'S CHRISTMAS DRAWINGS, Thomas Nast. Almost all Christmas drawings by creator of image of Santa Claus as we know it, and one of America's foremost illustrators and political cartoonists. 66 illustrations. 3 illustrations in color on covers. 96pp. 8⅜ x 11¼. 23660-9 Pa. $3.50

FRENCH COUNTRY COOKING FOR AMERICANS, Louis Diat. 500 easy-to-make, authentic provincial recipes compiled by former head chef at New York's Fitz-Carlton Hotel: onion soup, lamb stew, potato pie, more. 309pp. 5⅜ x 8½. 23665-X Pa. $3.95

SAUCES, FRENCH AND FAMOUS, Louis Diat. Complete book gives over 200 specific recipes: bechamel, Bordelaise, hollandaise, Cumberland, apricot, etc. Author was one of this century's finest chefs, originator of vichyssoise and many other dishes. Index. 156pp. 5⅜ x 8. 23663-3 Pa. $2.95

TOLL HOUSE TRIED AND TRUE RECIPES, Ruth Graves Wakefield. Authentic recipes from the famous Mass. restaurant: popovers, veal and ham loaf, Toll House baked beans, chocolate cake crumb pudding, much more. Many helpful hints. Nearly 700 recipes. Index. 376pp. 5⅜ x 8½. 23560-2 Pa. $4.95

ILLUSTRATED GUIDE TO SHAKER FURNITURE, Robert Meader. Director, Shaker Museum, Old Chatham, presents up-to-date coverage of all furniture and appurtenances, with much on local styles not available elsewhere. 235 photos. 146pp. 9 x 12. 22819-3 Pa. $6.95

COOKING WITH BEER, Carole Fahy. Beer has as superb an effect on food as wine, and at fraction of cost. Over 250 recipes for appetizers, soups, main dishes, desserts, breads, etc. Index. 144pp. 5⅜ x 8½. (Available in U.S. only) 23661-7 Pa. $3.00

STEWS AND RAGOUTS, Kay Shaw Nelson. This international cookbook offers wide range of 108 recipes perfect for everyday, special occasions, meals-in-themselves, main dishes. Economical, nutritious, easy-to-prepare: goulash, Irish stew, boeuf bourguignon, etc. Index. 134pp. 5⅜ x 8½. 23662-5 Pa. $3.95

DELICIOUS MAIN COURSE DISHES, Marian Tracy. Main courses are the most important part of any meal. These 200 nutritious, economical recipes from around the world make every meal a delight. "I . . . have found it so useful in my own household,"—N.Y. Times. Index. 219pp. 5⅜ x 8½. 23664-1 Pa. $3.95

FIVE ACRES AND INDEPENDENCE, Maurice G. Kains. Great back-to-the-land classic explains basics of self-sufficient farming: economics, plants, crops, animals, orchards, soils, land selection, host of other necessary things. Do not confuse with skimpy faddist literature; Kains was one of America's greatest agriculturalists. 95 illustrations. 397pp. 5⅜ x 8½. 20974-1 Pa. $4.95

A PRACTICAL GUIDE FOR THE BEGINNING FARMER, Herbert Jacobs. Basic, extremely useful first book for anyone thinking about moving to the country and starting a farm. Simpler than Kains, with greater emphasis on country living in general. 246pp. 5⅜ x 8½. 23675-7 Pa. $3.95

PAPERMAKING, Dard Hunter. Definitive book on the subject by the foremost authority in the field. Chapters dealing with every aspect of history of craft in every part of the world. Over 320 illustrations. 2nd, revised and enlarged (1947) edition. 672pp. 5⅜ x 8½. 23619-6 Pa. $8.95

THE ART DECO STYLE, edited by Theodore Menten. Furniture, jewelry, metalwork, ceramics, fabrics, lighting fixtures, interior decors, exteriors, graphics from pure French sources. Best sampling around. Over 400 photographs. 183pp. 8⅜ x 11¼. 22824-X Pa. $6.95

ACKERMANN'S COSTUME PLATES, Rudolph Ackermann. Selection of 96 plates from the Repository of Arts, best published source of costume for English fashion during the early 19th century. 12 plates also in color. Captions, glossary and introduction by editor Stella Blum. Total of 120pp. 8⅜ x 11¼. 23690-0 Pa. $5.00

CATALOGUE OF DOVER BOOKS

THE ANATOMY OF THE HORSE, George Stubbs. Often considered the great masterpiece of animal anatomy. Full reproduction of 1766 edition, plus prospectus; original text and modernized text. 36 plates. Introduction by Eleanor Garvey. 121pp. 11 x 14¾.   23402-9 Pa. $8.95

BRIDGMAN'S LIFE DRAWING, George B. Bridgman. More than 500 illustrative drawings and text teach you to abstract the body into its major masses, use light and shade, proportion; as well as specific areas of anatomy, of which Bridgman is master. 192pp. 6½ x 9¼. (Available in U.S. only)
22710-3 Pa. $4.50

ART NOUVEAU DESIGNS IN COLOR, Alphonse Mucha, Maurice Verneuil, Georges Auriol. Full-color reproduction of *Combinaisons ornementales* (c. 1900) by Art Nouveau masters. Floral, animal, geometric, interlacings, swashes—borders, frames, spots—all incredibly beautiful. 60 plates, hundreds of designs. 9⅜ x 8-1/16.   22885-1 Pa. $4.50

FULL-COLOR FLORAL DESIGNS IN THE ART NOUVEAU STYLE, E. A. Seguy. 166 motifs, on 40 plates, from *Les fleurs et leurs applications decoratives* (1902): borders, circular designs, repeats, allovers, "spots." All in authentic Art Nouveau colors. 48pp. 9⅜ x 12¼.
23439-8 Pa. $6.00

A DIDEROT PICTORIAL ENCYCLOPEDIA OF TRADES AND IN-DUSTRY, edited by Charles C. Gillispie. 485 most interesting plates from the great French Encyclopedia of the 18th century show hundreds of working figures, artifacts, process, land and cityscapes; glassmaking, paper-making, metal extraction, construction, weaving, making furniture, clothing, wigs, dozens of other activities. Plates fully explained. 920pp. 9 x 12.
22284-5, 22285-3 Clothbd., Two-vol. set $50.00

HANDBOOK OF EARLY ADVERTISING ART, Clarence P. Hornung. Largest collection of copyright-free early and antique advertising art ever compiled. Over 6,000 illustrations, from Franklin's time to the 1890's for special effects, novelty. Valuable source, almost inexhaustible.
Pictorial Volume. Agriculture, the zodiac, animals, autos, birds, Christmas, fire engines, flowers, trees, musical instruments, ships, games and sports, much more. Arranged by subject matter and use. 237 plates. 288pp. 9 x 12.
20122-8 Clothbd. $15.95

Typographical Volume. Roman and Gothic faces ranging from 10 point to 300 point, "Barnum," German and Old English faces, script, logotypes, scrolls and flourishes, 1115 ornamental initials, 67 complete alphabets, more. 310 plates. 320pp. 9 x 12.   20123-6 Clothbd. $16.95

CALLIGRAPHY (CALLIGRAPHIA LATINA), J. G. Schwandner. High point of 18th-century ornamental calligraphy. Very ornate initials, scrolls, borders, cherubs, birds, lettered examples. 172pp. 9 x 13.
20475-8 Pa. $7.95

GEOMETRY, RELATIVITY AND THE FOURTH DIMENSION, Rudolf Rucker. Exposition of fourth dimension, means of visualization, concepts of relativity as Flatland characters continue adventures. Popular, easily followed yet accurate, profound. 141 illustrations. 133pp. 5⅜ x 8½.
23400-2 Pa. $2.75

THE ORIGIN OF LIFE, A. I. Oparin. Modern classic in biochemistry, the first rigorous examination of possible evolution of life from nitrocarbon compounds. Non-technical, easily followed. Total of 295pp. 5⅜ x 8½.
60213-3 Pa. $5.95

PLANETS, STARS AND GALAXIES, A. E. Fanning. Comprehensive introductory survey: the sun, solar system, stars, galaxies, universe, cosmology; quasars, radio stars, etc. 24pp. of photographs. 189pp. 5⅜ x 8½. (Available in U.S. only)
21680-2 Pa. $3.75

THE THIRTEEN BOOKS OF EUCLID'S ELEMENTS, translated with introduction and commentary by Sir Thomas L. Heath. Definitive edition. Textual and linguistic notes, mathematical analysis, 2500 years of critical commentary. Do not confuse with abridged school editions. Total of 1414pp. 5⅜ x 8½.   60088-2, 60089-0, 60090-4 Pa., Three-vol. set $19.50

Prices subject to change without notice.

Available at your book dealer or write for free catalogue to Dept. GI, Dover Publications, Inc., 31 East 2nd St. Mineola., N.Y. 11501. Dover publishes more than 175 books each year on science, elementary and advanced mathematics, biology, music, art, literary history, social sciences and other areas.